The Ideology of Power in NATO Military Discourse

Studies in Military Psychology and Pedagogy

Edited by Hermann Jung / Hubert Annen

Vol. 16

PETER LANG

Isabela-Anda Dragomir

The Ideology of Power in NATO Military Discourse

A Proposed Analytical Framework

PETER LANG

Bibliographic Information published by the Deutsche Nationalbibliothek
The Deutsche Nationalbibliothek lists this publication in the Deutsche Nationalbibliografie; detailed bibliographic data is available online at http://dnb.d-nb.de.

Library of Congress Cataloging-in-Publication Data
A CIP catalog record for this book has been applied for at the Library of Congress.

ISSN 1619-778X
ISBN 978-3-631-89317-3 (Print)
E-ISBN 978-3-631-89318-0 (E-PDF)
E-ISBN 978-3-631-89319-7 (EPUB)
DOI 10.3726/b20599

© Peter Lang GmbH
Internationaler Verlag der Wissenschaften
Berlin 2023
All rights reserved.

Peter Lang – Berlin · Bruxelles · Lausanne · New York · Oxford

www.peterlang.de

Contents

1 Critical discourse analysis: between theory and method

The first definition of CDA is that it is, at the same time, a theoretical approach and a set of methods. Linguists who are interested in investigating the relationship between society and language use CDA as a method to assist them in describing, interpreting, and explaining such interconnectedness. CDA is not essentially different from other methods of discourse analysis but differs from them in that, in addition to describing and interpreting discourse in context, it also justifies as to how and why discourses function.

The terms "Critical Discourse Analysis" and "Critical Linguistics" are habitually used interchangeably. The term "CDA" has lately been used to stand for the theory previously identified as Critical Linguistics (CL). CDA regards "language as social practice" (Fairclough and Wodak 1997) and considers the context in which the language is used to be essential (Wodak 2000). Nowadays, the term "CDA" is used to talk about the critical approach of linguistic specialists who consider the broader discursive segment of text as being the elementary component of communication. Since CDA "has its origins in textual and linguistic analysis" (Hidalgo Tenorio 2011, par. 2), it is essential to perceive this method through the filter of Michael Halliday's Systemic Functional Grammar, which lies at the very foundation of discourse analysis and has been extensively used by practitioners in the field of CDA. Moreover, linguistics is not the only guidance on the evolution of CDA, as the theoretical grounds of this method are rooted in sociology, social theory, and philosophy.

1.1. An overview of CDA

The scholarly triumph of CDA does not come as a surprise. At the onset of *Discourse in Late Modernity,* authors Lilie Chouliaraki and Norman Fairclough argue:

> Critical discourse analysis...has established itself internationally over the past twenty years or so as a field of crossdisciplinary. teaching and research which has been widely drawn upon in the social sciences and the humanities (for example,

in sociology, geography, history and media studies), and has inspired critical language teaching at various levels and in various domains. (1999:1)

CDA developed in the last years of the 1980s as a programmatic evolution of research in European discourse studies fronted by linguists such as Teun A. Van Dijk, Ruth Wodak, Norman Fairclough, etc. Experts in the field of CDA have been trying to decipher and infer the meaning of a text in relation to the context (Van Dijk 2009; Van Leeuwen 2009; Widdowson 2004). Language is examined and defined as a social process in direct relation to the context, whose further interpretation helps determine the meaning of a statement for both the producer and the receiver. Furthermore, discourse analysts have enthusiastically explored and pinpointed the fundamental objective of meaning, that of entailing an ideological message based on sociopolitical, historical, and religious conventions (Blommaert and Verschueren 1998; Chilton 2004; Cameron 2001; Wodak 1989). CDA practitioners have actively trailed discursive practices of ideological impositions, power dominance, and discrimination, as transmitted through text and talk (Fairclough 2001; Van Dijk 2003b; Reisigl and Wodak 2005). Narrative analysis, conversation analysis, stylistics, rhetoric, and media analysis are just some of the methods put forward by experts in the field of CDA. The underlying approach may be used to analyze the discourse of speeches delivered by well-known politicians, parliamentarians, and national leaders.

According to the orientation, discipline, or paradigm involved, the development of CDA as a method of linguistic analysis can be mapped out as originating in the theories of the Enlightenment philosophers, of Marx or of the affiliates of the Frankfurt school (Benjamin, Adorno). After the 1960s, Jürgen Habermas can be nominated as a primary representative (Jay 1973; Slater 1977; Geuss 1981), while Stuart Hall and other members of the CCCS (Centre for Contemporary Cultural Studies) are to be mentioned as followers of Antonio Gramsci's Marxist philosophies on sociology and linguistics in France and in the UK. Other European and American influences in the 1970s and 1980s can be attributed to the works of Louis Althusser, Michel Foucault, and Michel Pêcheux, among others.

Discourse analysts are fundamentally aware of their role in society. Rejecting the existence of a "value-free" science, their main argument is that discourse, in all its forms, is part of a social structure and therefore influenced by it. Consequently, the interpretations, explanations, and descriptions produced by CDA are inherently socially and politically situated. According to Van Dijk, a critical investigation of discourse relies on a series of prerequisites:

> As is often the case for more marginal research traditions, CDA research has to be 'better' than other research in order to be accepted. It focuses primarily on *social problems* and political issues, rather than on current paradigms and fashions. Empirically adequate critical analysis of social problems is usually *multidisciplinary*. Rather than merely *describing* discourse structures, it tries to *explain* them in terms of properties of social interaction and especially social structure. More specifically, CDA focuses on the ways discourse structures enact, confirm, legitimate, reproduce, or challenge relations of *power* and *dominance* in society. (2003a:353)

CDA is not considered to be a precise direction of study, and consequently lacks a unitary theoretical framework. Against the background offered by the requirements above, CDA can split into diverse theoretical and analytical ramifications. Some methods focus on the context that generates the discourse and are consequently less linguistically linked. Others take into view the historical circumstances from which ideologies arise. There are methods that pay equal attention to language and social theory. Regardless of the chosen direction of analysis, "one of the major challenges of CDA is to make explicit the relations between discourse and knowledge" (Van Dijk 2003b:85). For the purpose of the current investigation, the starting point has been the generally accepted assumption that discourse and knowledge are both multifarious phenomena, extensively investigated in a myriad of disciplines, mainly humanities and social sciences. My approach is based on a theory of their relationship against the backdrop of intertwined linguistic, psychological, sociological, and philosophical aspects.

The philosophical enquiry dwells on the fundamental definition of the nature of knowledge, conventionally known as "justified true beliefs." Seen from an epistemological angle, communicative events materialized as situated talk or text are the only instances of communication that can be assessed as true or false, when, e.g., the values, beliefs, and attitudes they transmit are directly linked to reality. They obtain the "truth" dimension only when discursively declared.

Knowledge has traditionally been overlooked by linguistics; in compensation, cognitive grammar regards it as an important dimension of communication (Langacker 1983; Fauconnier 1985). Generative grammar refers to knowledge as the implicit awareness of the (rules of) grammar, commonly known and used by the members of a language community. Cognitive linguistics focuses on the importance of semantics and their close relations to the linguistic forms that convey meaning, exploring the linkage between knowledge and meaning and interpreting meaning in terms of conceptualization. Cognitive linguists do not view meaning as models of the world; instead, they construct it as mental spaces, as idealized cognitive models, in which construction of meaning involves semantic frames not necessarily congruent with reality (Faucounnier and Turner 2003; Geeraerts 2006; Geeraerts and Cuyckens 2007).

The concept of "knowledge about knowledge," described as cognitive representations located in human memory, has been extensively dealt with in psychology (Britton and Graesser 1996; Markman 1999; Van Dijk and Kintsch 1983; Schank and Abelson 1977). Producing and understanding discourse involves complex procedures related to the way in which meaning, form, and action are managed. This process involves extensive knowledge: for example, concepts such as topics, implication, presuppositions, schematic structures, global and local coherence, other properties of discourse, all entail a knowledge component. In the case of the current investigation, the interpretation of military discourse requires a knowledge component, necessary to understand both its meaning and its forms.

A significant number of present-day studies in discourse studies and pragmatics have shown that knowledge is, at the same time, mental and social (Potter 1996; Fairclough and Wodak 1997). Knowledge is assimilated, shared, used, and recycled by people who interact, which are individuals or members of different groups, institutions, and organizations. In the absence of a collective, socially shared foundation, knowledge would only be defined as personal belief. In its social dimension, knowledge is transmitted and acquired through communication (talk and text), through the situated discourse of social institutions (the media, governments, institutions of education, and the military). The mechanism of comprehension is facilitated by consensus, common sense, or common ground (Clark

1996). These socially constructed characteristics define presuppositions, delineate implicatures, eliminate misinterpretations, and allow a shared understanding of the discourse, since relevant knowledge does not need to be made explicit all the time.

The epistemic foundation that facilitates discourse construction and comprehension needs an explicit definition in terms of culture. Scholars are united in the belief that the cultural dimension of knowledge is essential (D'Andrade 1995; Holland and Quin 1987; Shore 1996). The concept of knowledge shared by a group or by an institution can also be tackled in terms of "culture." Epistemic communities are defined as collectivities or organizations, as "communities of practice, thought and discourse" (Van Dijk 2003b:86). Different disciplines have successfully married the social and the cognitive dimensions of knowledge, and CDA is no exception. This joint perspective can be applied in research related to military culture and discourse, an extremely fertile territory where the exploration of such an integration will definitely yield a rich crop.

Parallel observations can be applied to the notion of discourse, which has multifaceted dimensions, which include philosophical, linguistic, cognitive, social, cultural, and historical aspects. Consequently, the relation between discourse and knowledge can be explored from a multidisciplinary perspective. Knowledge and discourse are intertwined: knowledge makes possible the production and understanding of discourse; the acquisition of knowledge often necessitates discourse. The conclusion that socially significant knowledge is normally reproduced in text and talks logically follows this train of thought.

1.2. The "critical" dimension of discourse analysis

In building a theoretical framework of CDA, it is necessary to answer some questions, as to draft a general view of the concepts that go into the definition of CDA as a method of content analysis: Why *critical?* What is *discourse?* What does *analysis* mean in this context?

The notion of *criticality*, which draws from the influence of Jurgen Habermas or the Frankfurt School is, however, conservatively employed in a more comprehensive sense designating, in Hermann Krings's words, the practical connection between "social and political engagement" and "a sociologically informed construction of society" (Krings et al. 1973:808). Fairclough also argues: "In human matters, interconnections and chains of cause and effect may be distorted out of vision." Therefore, "critique" is basically directed toward "making visible the interconnectedness of things" (1985:747).

Wodak and Meyer define CDA as "essentially concerned with examining opaque as well as transparent structural relationships of discrimination, dominance, power and control, as manifested in language" (2009:2). The main goal of CDA is to critically examine social disparity as it is conveyed, flagged, created, and validated by the use of language through discourse. Most critical discourse scholars validate Habermas's assertion that "language is also a medium of domination and social force. It serves to legitimize relations of organized power. In so far as the legitimations of power relations...are not articulated...language is also ideological" (1977:259).

Unlike other hypotheses championed in text linguistics and in discourse analysis, CDA focuses on text and talk, i.e., spoken, or written texts, perceived as objects of investigation, and also operationalizes and describes the social processes and structures involved in the construction of a text. The main focus is on those specific social processes and structures within which individuals or groups generate meanings as a consequence of their interaction with texts. Consequently, three concepts have been established as essential in CDA: *power*, *history*, and *ideology*. Accordingly, and although the linguistic manifestations of power dynamics constitute the main focus of this monograph, no investigative journey into the realm of military discourse can flout the tripartite relation that comprises history and ideology.

The *critical* dimension of CDA also refers to its goal to explain and interpret the connection between the form and function of the language. The form of language consists of morphology, semantics, syntax, and pragmatics. The function of language refers to how people use the language to achieve a communicational outcome in different situations. Based on the relationship existing between the form and the function of the language, it is only natural to assume that certain networks of form-function relations are preferred by the military over others; this postulation entails an explanation as to why certain patterns are more valued than others and what makes them so. In the light of the belief that structures of meaning are related to socially established practices that are relatively valued or privileged in the society, the present exploration focuses on the relation between language and power, as manifested in the military discourse. In the words of Chouliaraki and Fairclough, "the links between particular discourses and social positions and, therefore, the ideological effects of discourse are established and negotiated in the process of articulation within a practice" (1999:150). Against this backdrop, the implication of criticality is that "although ideology inevitably exists, it is explicitly studied" (Rogers 2004:4).

1.3. The fundamental triad: discourse, text, and context

With CDA being most commonly defined as "problem-oriented social research, founded in social history, semiotics and linguistics" (Hidalgo Tenorio 2011: par. 1), it is important to clarify the concept of *discourse*, commonly used in association with other two terms: *text* and *context*.

There are various definitions to the concept of *discourse*. The taxonomy by Bloor and Bloor defines *discourse* as:

1. the highest unit of linguistic description; phonemes, morphemes, words, phrases, clauses, sentences, and texts are subunits;
2. a sample of language usage, generally written to be spoken, i.e., a speech;
3. referring to the communication expected in one situation context, alongside one field and register, such as the discourse of law or medicine;
4. human interaction through any means, verbal and non-verbal;
5. spoken interaction only;
6. the whole communicative event. (2007:6–7)

It is obvious that *discourse* is seen in different ways by various researchers and differs depending on the academic cultures defining it. The English-speaking world uses the term "discourse" for written and oral texts, meaning both text and talk (Schiffrin 1992). Different levels of abstractness are also distinguished. In line with Foucault's epistemic approaches, Jay L. Lemke's (1995) definition describes *text* as the materialization of abstract structures of knowledge (*discourse*). Wodak's discourse-historical approach enlarges the concept and relates to Van Dijk's sociocognitive theory, and defines *discourse* as manifestations of knowledge, in opposition to the notion of *text*, which encapsulates written documents and/or concrete oral utterances (Wodak 2001). Fairclough views *discourse* as "a way of signifying a particular domain of social practice from a particular perspective" (1995:14). In Wodak's view, CDA starts the investigation from the premise that there is a dialectical link between specific discursive practices and the particular domains of action (situations, social frames, and social structures) where they manifest.

> The situational, institutional, and social settings shape and affect discourses, but discourses equally influence both discursive and non-discursive social and political processes and actions. In other words, discourses as linguistic social practices can be seen as constituting non-discursive and discursive social practices and, at the same time, as being constituted by them. (2000, par. 1)

James Paul Gee (1999) makes a clear-cut separation between *small-d (discourse)* and *big-D (Discourse)*. The former refers to text and talk, broken down into the small components known as language bits, or, in other words, the grammar of what is said. The latter encapsulates the knowledge that is created and transmitted in talk. The same author's definition of *Discourse* refers to the systems of judgments, social conventions, and conversation patterns that typify a particular field, to the way of observing the world and behaving accordingly, and, finally, to the actions that go in the construction of social practices.

The same line of conceptualization is also followed by Paul Chilton's (2004) definitions of *language-L, language-l, discourse-D* and *discourse-d*. He does not focus his analyses on the practical aspects of language, i.e., structure and lexicon, but lays emphasis on the investigation of *context*, which is, in his opinion, a completely subjective interpretation of reality, construed as "representations of the mind and accessed when presumed relevant" (155). His approach lands on the theories put forward by cognitive linguistics, establishing the role of the language in communicating representations of the world.

Deborah Cameron's (2001) delineation is analogous and differentiates between the *linguists' discourse* and the *social theorists' discourse(s)*, making a definite distinction between what is known as language beyond the sentence level and language in use. Very much in the same line, Van Dijk (1997) suggests definitions that encapsulate linguistic, cognitive, and sociocultural dimensions, describing discourse at the semantic, syntactic, stylistic, and rhetorical levels. The second proposition of the same author is to understand discourse from the perspective of the speakers' processes of construction, assimilation, and understanding of the language in use. The two views are supplemented with a third dimension, i.e., the social dimension, described as a sequential system of organized, purposeful, and contextualized actions, performed in society, occurring in contextualized settings (physical, temporal) and involving social actors (the participants). Starting from the premise that context is mainly cognition, socially linked with the knowledge of situations and institutions, and governs the manner in which language is used, I endorse the author's claim that contexts control specific types of discourse and that discourses are in turn dependent on specific contexts.

H.G. Widdowson (2004) distinguishes between two types of texts (i.e., written and spoken). In the author's view, texts have an inherent linguistic component and must be labeled in terms of their purpose and intention. Alternatively, discourse, defined as text in context, is "the pragmatic process of meaning negotiation, while text is its product" (8). Since co-textual relations characterize texts, and contextual relations link back to discourse, it is natural to assume that text cohesion and discourse coherence are characterized by a relation of interdependency.

The broad understanding of "text" as a late modern concept is, in Fairclough's analysis, synonymous with "discourse" as an abstract noun: it includes verbal (i.e., spoken and written language) and nonverbal semiotic elements (i.e., gestures and images).

> "Text" or "discourse" is one of the four major categories of elements (physical, sociological, cultural/psychological and text) or "moments" of social practice, which must be seen in a dialectical relationship, in processes of "articulation" (he cites Laclau and Mouffe) during which each element is transformed through the mediation of the generative powers of the others. (2000:169)

It is in this dialectical relationship that "text" can be analyzed, according to case, as contributing to the construction of social life and social change, respectively. From the same author's perspective, "text" gains a "generative power," the force to "socially produce, i.e., to work, in its textual moment" (169).

Against this theoretical background, the concept of *context* emerges as being intricately related to the definition of discourse. Weiss and Wodak give a four-level definition of *context*. They explain:

The first level is descriptive, while the other three levels are part of our theories on context:

1. the immediate, language or text internal co-text;
2. the intertextual and interdiscursive relationship between utterances, texts, genres, and discourses;
3. the extralinguistic social/sociological variables and institutional frames of a specific context of situation (middle-range theories);
4. the broader sociopolitical and historical contexts, which the discursive practices are embedded in and related to. (2007:67)

There is neither a simple nor a final answer to a question inquiring about the investigative nature of CDA. *Analysis* greatly depends on what the researcher has taken up as definitions of *critical* and *discourse*. It is also dictated by the purpose of the analysis and the intentions of the researcher. This results in various and more or less textually oriented methods of analysis. In conclusion, considering the wide array of conceptual delimitations and theoretical approaches to this method, I argue that there is no fixed formula for doing CDA. I believe that it is the researchers' duty to choose the entry point of their analysis, and to carefully consider the three dimensions of CDA described above (critical, discourse, and analysis).

1.4. CDA at the intersection of three interdisciplinary approaches

Of the scholars who have placed great emphasis on the interdisciplinary dimension of CDA, the most noteworthy and relevant for my research have proven to be Teun A. Van Dijk, Norman Fairclough, and Ruth Wodak, each with their unique and valuable contribution to the trans-, cross-, and multidisciplinary expansion of CDA.

Fairclough's *Dialectical-Relational Approach* is focused on his research (1995, 2001) of the three main tenets of CDA: language, ideology, and power. Fairclough is interested in exploring the semiotic reproduction of social issues in discourse, with emphasis on social processes (including social structures, practices, and events). Fairclough describes the main center of this methodology as being "a contribution to the general rising of consciousness of exploitative social relations, through focusing upon language" (2001:4). Chouliaraki and Fairclough maintain that this approach "brings social science and linguistics...together within a single theoretical and analytical framework, setting up a dialogue between them" (1999:6). The two authors also claim: "The past two decades or so have been a period of profound economic social transformation on a global scale" (30). They posit that the recent economic, social, and political changes are actually transformations in the language and discourse. With such an objective in mind, the proposed critical analysis of military communication is intended to demonstrate that the linguistic features of a communication event are logically linked to what happens in the society, thus bridging the gap between ideology and discourse. In line with Fairclough's approach of CDA, this investigation also proposes a three-fold deconstruction of any communicative event: *text, discourse practice,* and *sociocultural practice.*

These three elements are consistent with Van Dijk's three-dimensional analysis of ideology, whose *Socio-Cognitive Discourse Analysis* incorporates *discourse, sociocognition,* and *social analysis.* This method is defined as an approach investigating the intersections between cognition, discourse, and society. In Van Dijk's approach, social knowledge and cognitive models mediate between discourse and social analysis, while Fairclough considers that discourse practices (text production and consumption) are key in managing the relation of the two. Cognition, the key element in Van Dijk's methodology, is achieved "in collective mental models as a result of consensus and becomes the interface between societal and discourse structures" (2009:63). Based on the guidelines set by the above-mentioned approaches, I also agree with the fact that there is a dialectical connection between societal structures and discursive interaction. Against this background, discourse is the medium by which societal organizations are "enacted, instituted, legitimated, confirmed or challenged by text and talk" (Fairclough and Wodak 1997:266). Serge Moscovici's

(2000) social representation theory is the foundation of Van Dijk's model of context presented in his 2009 "Critical Discourse Studies" article: social actors involved in discourse do not exclusively make use of their individual experiences, but rely upon collective frames of perception known as social representations, a bulk of the values, norms, concepts, explanations, and images shared in a social group, and activated and maintained in discourse. The proposed framework of analysis investigates local meanings, formal structures, semantic macrostructures, local and global discourse forms, and linguistic realizations in particular contexts. Coherence, rhetorical figures, speech acts, propositional structures, and lexical and topic selection implications are some of the specific elements that are explored from the perspective of Van Dijk's *Cognitive Discourse Analysis*.

Wodak focuses on discourse sociolinguistics from a historical perspective. Her approach locates and explains the fundamental mechanisms that fuel disorders of discourse, rooted in a particular context, and manifested at a specific moment, which inevitably affect communication. Wodak's approach, which she labeled the *Discourse-Historical Method,* stems from her 1990s analysis of the discourse centered on anti-Semitism. A central place in this approach is occupied by the term *historical,* denoting the scholar's attempt to systematically incorporate the accessible background information in the study of the many levels of discourse. As a result, the approach designed by Wodak and her colleagues in Vienna is based on the conclusion that the context of the discourse greatly impacts on the structure, function, and production of the communicative event. This method is grounded on the belief that "language manifests social processes and interaction while simultaneously generating those specific processes" (Wodak and Ludwig 1999:12). This method analyzes language from a three-fold perspective: first, the assumption that discourse is a communicative embodiment of power and ideologies. "No interaction exists where power relations do not prevail and where values and norms do not have a relevant role" (12). The second hypothesis argues that "discourse ... is always historical, that is, it is connected synchronically and diachronically with other communicative events which are happening at the same time, or which have happened before" (12). Third, Wodak's approach is centered on the concept of interpretation. The same two authors postulate that the social actors involved in the discourse (the readers and the listeners alike) might interpret the same communicative event differently, based on their background knowledge, available information, and role. DHA distinguishes four interrelated models of context, all based on understanding historical knowledge "at the level of the linguistic co-text, at the intertextual and interdiscursive level, at the extralinguistic level, and finally at the socio-political and historical level" (Wodak and Meyer 2009:29). The linguistic intersection between texts and discourses can be deconstructed with the help of notions such as *decontextualization* and *recontextualisation*, by which archetypal elements characterizing a specific context can be extracted from it and re-implanted into a new context, without there being a previous association between them. As a method, DHA has generated a variety of analytical and descriptive instruments, mainly utilized for the localization of ideologies (nomination, predication, argumentation, perspectivisation, intensification and mitigation). These are subsumed to a wider procedure of analysis that involves, among others, the description of the content of a discourse, the analysis of the linguistic methods of communication, and the context-related realizations of stereotypes. One of the strong points of this approach is the utilization of an abductive approach, a continuous movement between application and theoretical guidelines.

CDA is still at the dawn of its existence as a discipline. Curiously enough, as "unripe" as it might be considered, its critical stimulated the development of new approaches, aimed at raising awareness about social, political, religious, etc. issues nowadays. Nonetheless, both supporters and opponents of CDA often recognize its asymmetry and are united in acknowledging that it is directed mostly to linguists with an interest in critical analysis and not to the ordinary people in the street.

Drawbacks notwithstanding, CDA established itself as a method worthy of using, with a well-defined role in social sciences. The approach targets the construction and deconstruction of discourses, explores the allegiance of the participants in communication to collective social institutions, and proposes to ultimately analyze the discursive means by which the reality is interpreted and understood.

2 Military communication

Communication is key to the effective functioning of any organization, be it military or civilian, on a global scale. It is often advisable that communication, especially in the military context, be perceived and managed extremely carefully so that the armed forces be permitted to exert their role regionally, nationally, and internationally as part of the partnership programs they are involved in. Communication influences and is influenced by all organizational processes and phenomena: organizational culture, decision-making style, leadership style, conflict mediation, conflict mitigation, organizational changes, and evolution of the organization.[1]

2.1. Communication in the military organization

Throughout its history, the military organization has aimed at permanently improving communication in order to achieve competitive superiority at all levels. In the context of the asymmetrical warfare defining the types of conflicts in the 21st century, the concept of military communication has gained paramount importance, emerging as a sine-qua-non instrument for transmitting not only orders, commands (at the level of the micro-organization), strategies, and doctrines (at macro level) but also ideologies (in society), encompassed in the very fabric of the discourse.

A number of factors are being recognized as being able to both facilitate and hinder communication, implicitly affecting the operative efficiency

---

1 The issue of military communication has been previously approached from an institutional as well as from an international perspective in the article *Communication in the Military Organization: An Illustration of Facts,* published in the Journal of Communication and Development Studies, The Papua New Guinea University of Technology, Vol. III–IV, 2016–2017, pp. 51–58, ISSN 1992–1322. Further research was materialized in a conference presentation with the title *Military communication in intercultural contexts,* subsequently published in the Proceedings of the International Conference "Globalization, Intercultural Dialogue and National Identity", 3rd Edition, Arhipelag XXI Press, Târgu Mureş, 19–20 May 2016 (Iulian Boldea, Coord.), pp. 982–995, ISBN 978-606-8624-03-7.

of the military as a system. Among these, Nicolae Rotaru identifies as follows: the national and international context that shapes communication within the military organization; sociological aspects that influence the efficiency of the military; psychological elements that create the circumstances for productive communication; methods of increasing psychological sensitivity to communication-related issues; the need to learn foreign languages, stemming from the increasingly prominent role of the military in extra-national contexts (2005:31).

2.1.1. External influences

Before drawing a descriptive framework of military communication, it is purposive to analyze the external factors, both national and international, that can influence – in a positive or in a negative manner – the effectiveness of communication itself. These can be enumerated as follows: historical traditions, geopolitical context, international policies, socioeconomic aspects.

One essential element that significantly subsidizes the efficiency of communication within the military organization is history. Soldiers and civilians are united in recognizing the role and influence exerted by the military throughout the existence of any country, acknowledging the army as a major contributor to the greatness and solid positioning acquired by all representative state institutions. As a consequence, communication within the organization and also between the organization and the civil state rests unchallenged from the outside and implicitly gains effectiveness and functionality.

The geopolitical context also dictates the way in which communication is perceived, in its dimension of provider of information within the organization and also outside its borders. Since Rudolf Kjellen coined the term "geopolitics" in 1899, military representatives, analysts, specialists, commentators, and observers have invoked its semantics in order to connect the political to the realities of the modern society. The new political and social orientations which bring to the forefront space-related issues such as regionalization, globalization, internationalization, and the new world order are many elements continuously shaping and tailoring the purpose and manifestations of organizational communication.

Intrinsically linked to geopolitical orientations are international policies, which, in addition to cooperation and mutual interests, also entail the urge to have an armed force ready to preserve and enforce them. In an international context, where the greater good prevails and all independent elements (i.e., states and member countries) are interwoven within the same fabric (i.e., international organizations, such as UN, NATO, EU), emphasis is laid on the awareness raised on the topic of collective defense, as a guarantor of world peace and security. Against this background, Christopher Boucek (2008) argues, the feeling of safety and the desire to protect the national and international assets (be they geographic, social, economic, demographic, etc.) attract the need to construct and maintain optimal communication levers inside and outside the military organization.

The socioeconomic conditions affecting the development of a country are not to be neglected. The civilian population from socially and economically advanced countries are increasingly manifesting a lack of resilience to budgeting the defense industry. The prolonged period of peace Europe has enjoyed for the last forty years has attenuated the need to have a strong, well-endowed army to act as deterrent to possible but unlikely conflicts. This has negatively affected communication within the military organization, which is currently compromised by the contradiction between the wish to attain a high level of operationalization and the economic restrictions which hamper this desideratum.[2]

2.1.2. Sociological aspects

Obviously, the structure, systems, and leadership styles influence communication and its manifestations in any organization (military, industrial, commercial). Nowadays, in the light of the modern technological and organizational revolution, the military organization is increasingly similar to civilian institutions; nonetheless, it differs in a radical way – its members must be always ready to pay the supreme sacrifice: their life. Due to this life-binding commitment, the military must act like a rigidly stratified

---

2   Achieving Sustainable Development and Promoting Development Cooperation
    Dialogues at the Economic and Social Council, 2008.

organization, in which each level is linked to its hierarchical superior or subordinate by immediate and loyal allegiance.

The organizational structure, as mentioned before, is strictly stratified. It manifests – formally and informally – through diverse attitudes, behaviors, conducts, and reactions between otherwise equal members of the society, classified and empowered by the institution according to rank and position. The hierarchy is rigid and must be obeyed under all circumstances, by all members of the organization, regardless of their race, color, status, age, gender, etc. When the hierarchical flow does not move smoothly across the organization, communication is obstructed. Therefore, it is of paramount importance that members of the military, at all levels of the chain of command, possess effective communicative skills, which they must be able to activate in order to fulfill the entrusted tasks, without dwelling on discriminative criteria other than their position in the hierarchy. Although it is not a sine-qua-non requirement of the military profession, the ability to communicate efficiently is a fundamental constituent of professional competence, particularly at higher levels. A problem easy to address and solve if Paul Grice's (1975) four maxims of communicative convention (quantity, quality, relevance, and manner) are respected. I argue that, consequently, dialogue and documents produced by the military as an organization must avoid imprecision, ambiguities, and implicatures. Communication, in virtue of all its roles and functions, needs to be constructed so as to circumvent linguistic, gesture, behavior, and attitude impreciseness and to transmit the message as clearly and efficiently as possible.

The aforementioned aspects become particularly important when the act of communication is defined by the leadership style. Taking into consideration that the military organization is mainly characterized by group work, cooperation, and coordination among isolated elements, it is critical that the level of communication between the members of the organization be optimal, a characteristic which falls under the responsibility of the leader, constantly concerned with facilitating clear and efficient transfer of information. As Constantin Afrim and Mircea Cosma argue in their 2015 book on efficient communication in military organizations, the inherent conditions of communication (transparency, freedom of expression, respect for others' opinions, positive feedback) are conscientiously respected by all the members of the organization and define modern military discourse.

2.1.3. Psychological factors

Communication is inherently human, and the human being, H.G. Gadamer (1994) claims, is a being in language. In this context, the communicative act is subsumed to psychological factors and conditioned by fundamental needs. By correlating Abraham Maslow's pyramid of human needs with the linguistic manifestations thereof, a dual classification of communication is obtained: nonverbal (voluntary and involuntary) and verbal (oral and written). I argue that both categories are manifested in the military organization, with different impact and results and that an overview of the notion of communication must comprise a short presentation of each.

Nonverbal communication includes non-linguistic means of expression and communication. It consists of "visual/kinetic clues, such as facial expressions, eye movement, gestures, and body orientations; vocal/paralinguistic cues, such as volume, pitch, rate, and inflection; proxemics cues such as space and distance; olfactory or smell cues; cues provided via artifactual communication and appearance; cues sent via colors; and chronemic or time cues" (Gamble 2013:152). All the elements included in the physical layout of a page account for the nonverbal dimension of written communication.

Members belonging to the same military organization or to different military organizations often resort to nonverbal instruments to communicate. This may occur in informal settings and contexts and between members of the global military organization who obviously do not share a common cultural background (as is the case with international coalitions and theaters of operations). However, as this book focuses on military discourse (oral and written), more attention will be placed on verbal communication. Suffice it to declare that, from a psychological angle, verbal expression entails using language as a means by which an individual communicates himself/herself, revealing or, conversely, dissimulating their intentions, attitude, opinion, feelings, etc. The ability to perceive both verbal and nonverbal communication is indispensable in any organization characterized by cooperation and teamwork, and the military makes no exception.

Against this backdrop, we can conclude that, from a broad perspective, communication in the modern military organization is characterized by several factors:

✓ The use of a common language, extremely important in the case of international cooperation and in the context of interoperability and standardization, is an essential prerequisite of fulfilling interoperable objectives in the modern military context. Furthermore, I aim to demonstrate that members of the military organization are aware of the need to correlate professional language, terminology, and jargon, in order for communication to take place efficiently and for the tasks to be understood correctly and applied effectively.

✓ Effective encoding and decoding techniques, stemming from the necessity that senders and receivers operate with the same interpretation parameters.

✓ Openness and tolerance between members of the chain of command at all hierarchical echelons and on both levels (horizontally and vertically). It is imperative that modern-time leaders listen to their subordinates and encourage creativity and exchange of ideas, while subordinates must overcome the prejudice of not being listened to, approved, or respected for their point of view.

✓ Effective communication techniques, by which the message is transmitted clearly, unequivocally, free of ambiguities, and interpretations beyond the actual meaning. I set out to investigate the discourse elements that make military communication straightforward, with simple but powerful words, whose unequivocal usage brings added value to the content of the message.

2.2. Linguistic aspects of military communication

The linguistic exploration of military communication proposed by this book aims at analyzing the specific verbal elements which transmit ideologies and the communication patterns specific thereof. A content analysis of the discourse as the main component of military communication will specifically target the study of language, generator and bearer of values, norms, beliefs, and ideology inherent to the military culture. In this context, in addition to language and as a component of military culture, the ideology inherent in military discourse is transferred with the help of specific elements: the system of values, symbols, verbal components, rituals and ceremonies, actors and heroes, physical elements.

The noteworthy features of military communication are particularly salient from the specific language used by the members of the organization (military and civilians alike). This distinct form of language is shaped by the role of the participants in the communication process, by the use of certain forms of communication, and by some specific means of transmitting the message. Military language is recognized as specialized language, the so-called military terminology, characterized by words and phrases specific to the organization as a whole and to separate military branches and specialties. In short, military language is materialized through linguistic formulas (specific terminology, abbreviations, acronyms, set phrases, slang, expressions, etc.) and by particular means of communication such as orders, reports, commands, etc. When analyzing the military environment, one cannot ignore the hierarchical, pyramid-type organization of the institution, the subordination relations, the existence of rules of conduct, the specific ways of addressing, reporting, etc.

In regard to the forms of communication used in the military organization, Afrim and Cosma (2015) mention the following: formal communication, vertical communication, oral communication, written communication. The four forms are not separately identifiable, but operate simultaneously, in parallel and in perfect osmosis, providing military communication increased efficiency and effectiveness in its dimension as linguistic communication. For example, formal communication, which has two sub-types, namely vertical communication (ascendant and descendant) and horizontal communication (between members of the organization situated on the same hierarchical level) can be achieved either in writing or orally, and has several functions: information, motivation, socializing, regulating actions, etc.

The method of dissemination used by the military in its relation to the civilian society is mass communication. It is particularly relevant from the perspective of its role – that of propagating military values and beliefs. The public opinion is informed in an institutionalized manner, and the methods preferred by the military include books, written media, radio broadcasts, televised interventions, and communications in virtual spaces, through the internet.

Linguistically, the act of communication in the military can also be scrutinized from an intercultural angle. Language is a finely articulated vehicle for the promotion of ideas, values, beliefs, attitudes, and ideologies, all of which are conjoined in what linguists call *discourse*, defined as "a social practice, a particular way of making meaning of experience" (Fairclough 1992:7). If we take the rationale even further, we can anchor the discourse in the sociocultural context in which it operates, thus enabling it to promote those particular ideas, values, beliefs, attitudes inherent to the ideology of the community it belongs to. Jay Lemke (1995) argues that the social nature of discourse and meaning making place this practice in particular communities that operate in particular sociocultural and political contexts. Therefore, we can speak of a *military discourse*, specific to this community of practice, with its own particular features and composition structures and patterns, genre, style, language, method of production, circulation, distribution, reception, and consumption, which is contextually, ideologically, organizationally, and globally shaped and controlled.

The most relevant terms which populate the political, strategic, and military communication from an ideological point of view emerge from discussions on the contemporary hot topics, debating the new world order, global security and stability; crisis management; and, more recently, combating terrorism, in the context of the fight for the "balance of power" and "imperialistic hegemony." Syntagms such as "credible retaliation," "real discouragement," "sustainability," "robust expansion," "common interest," "diplomatic soldier" are recurrently employed in the modern military discourse as adjuvants for the resuscitation of the values and beliefs promoted by international organizations, and they are aimed at discursively supporting the visions of the policy-makers and strategists who champion the idea of the "ultimate solution," i.e., a "military intervention," the involvement of a "force in being" that would provide security and offer an alternative to the state of "chaos" generated by the effects of the emergent crises. Contemporary conflicts necessitate "punitive measures" in order to deal with the "catastrophic terror" which require preventive-combative and humanitarian interventions, often described as "surgical," which ignore the traditional values on which the "weak" third world has based its existence: "sovereignty," "independence," "territorial integrity," "equality of rights," "self-fulfillment"; in the name of a "sustainable peace," frequently built on utopian scaffolds: "regionalization," "globalization," "internationalization," "collective defense," "collective security," "global government," "continental federalization," "global village," etc.

In the context of the more recent COVID-19 pandemic, the lexical choices used to describe the virus and the situation it created worldwide draw heavily on military vocabulary. In an interview with Radio Free Europe, given at the onset of the medical crisis of 2020, Romanian President Klaus Johannis declared that "we are in the midst of a full-fledged war for preserving humanity's health"; Russian media equates the virus with a weapon, titling: "New global weapons: coronavirus hits the West harder than Russia"; in issuing a 2021 public statement about the efforts of his government to mitigate the ravages of COVID-19, Australian Prime Minister Scott Morrison claimed that "this has been a long war against the virus, and there have been many, many battles"; just before falling victim to the virus himself, British Prime Minister Boris Johnson called his government into acting as a "wartime government" that has to fight a "deadly enemy" (Oneț and Ciocoi-Pop 2022).

2.3. Challenges for military communication in the current global context

Today, and more poignantly in the aftermath of the gloomy moment that radically reshaped global international communication, on September 11, 2001, Anatol Rapoport's (1960) taxonomy, which classifies conflicts into three types (fight, game, and debate), remains valid, actual, and yet subject to amendments dictated by the global context of the modern world. Defined in the 1960s, these three types have been since recognized as the main sorts of crisis underlying international conflicts, with implications pertaining to the nature and manifestations of communication. Experts in the field of military communication have found themselves challenged by several questions, all narrowing down to the same fundamental interrogation: "Is communication a source of conflict?" (Marcus 1985: Agabrian

1994; Bouzon 2006; Marin 2006). It has been argued that defective communication, or the lack thereof, is the actual cause of conflicts. Consequently, the military has invested all its institutional resources into transforming communication into an active diplomatic dialogue so as to nurture "the most sensible type of conflict: the debate" and demonstrate that "a world of peace is not a world without conflicts, but one in which conflicts do not generate wars" (Marcus 1985:138).

Successful communication depends, to a great extent, on the quality and fluidity of the communication cycle. Correct identification of the issue to be transmitted, clarity of the message, its linguistic formulation, the analysis of the reception of the message and its adaptation to the profile of the receiver, and the versatility of the strategies utilized in the process are all essential elements that ensure an efficient and optimal communication. In the words of Lionel Bellenger, "to communicate well means first of all to listen well" (1989:8). The truism according to which good communication involves good listening skills may seem redundant nowadays, but the dares of the modern world have indicated that the military institution needs to be open to the public opinion and continuously adapt to the security requirements stemming from the current political and social context.

Modern military communication is now challenged by the myriad of media enabling its manifestations: multimedia (text, data, graphs, sound, image, video, movement, voice, etc.), hypermedia (multimedia and associative media), and intelmedia systems (intelligence incorporated within hypermedia). These channels provide uninterrupted availability of information, mobility, flexibility, transparency, and diversity and facilitate the creation of credible areas for common space, common time, and common presence, within the borders of an interactive system of communication, in a geopolitical environment whose parameters are consistently shaped and reshaped by globalized communication.

From a functional perspective (resonant with the theories put forward by Plato, Comte, Spencer, Durkheim, and Merton), communication in the military environment is delineated by discursive patterns of influential and structural dependency that contribute to maintaining the social order, to alleviating imbalances, and to mitigating risks, vulnerabilities, threats, instability, conflicts, and confrontations. Against this background, professional communicators – diplomats, negotiators, politicians, military representatives – have been relentlessly striving to mitigate crises; to enhance and exploit the roles and functions of communication so as to exclude ambiguity, imprecision, misunderstandings, and suspicions from the military discourse; to encourage dialogue and transparency; and to nurture empathy and tolerance of perspectives and viewpoints. Moreover, regardless of the political and strategic orientations, communication is bound to fulfilling its role, that of conveying ideologies and connecting the bearers thereof through dialogue and exchange of ideas. In the modern world of global models, information is not only generated but also transmitted at a fast pace, and military 'products' of this kind need to be received and consumed accordingly.

Two of the more recent examples of social and political occurrences that have stamped on the configuration of public military discourse are the Covid-19 pandemic and the Russia-Ukraine conflict. The challenges brought about by these events are not only strategic but also communicational, as the large public has been quite aggressively exposed to a "militarized" rhetoric, aimed at raising the general public's awareness of the devastating effects of the two exemplified critical situations (the epidemic and the war).

The pandemic-generated discourse, which depicts the virus in typical war-like terms, was used by governments in the hope to awaken a sense of urgency and responsibility in the general population. By invoking notions of war and describing the virus as a "wicked enemy" (Ralph and Stoove 2021), international media harnessed the discursive power of military language, with the purpose of mobilizing the entire community to react in an emergency situation. This particular example is extremely useful in illustrating the power of language in swaying public opinion. Nonetheless, contrary to the desired effect, such alarmistic language and military metaphors only intimidated the audience and generated a feeling of pessimism and hopelessness in the face of the danger. Used as a manipulation tool during the coronavirus pandemic, military vocabulary only "increased anxiety levels" (Freshwater 2020) and nurtured the population's distrust in a positive outcome of the crisis.

At the opposite end of the spectrum lies NATO's own discourse. The Alliance's long tradition of communicating facts and maintaining an objective and balanced attitude toward critical events also transpired from the rhetoric used in the Organization's public documents during the COVID-19 crisis. For instance, the factsheet entitled "NATO's Response to the COVID-19 Pandemic" issued at the onset of the pandemic (February 2021) pivots on the concepts of support, help, cooperation, vigilance, readiness, all of which are directed at building and reinforcing trust among member states, partner nations, and international organizations. Through the power of language, the Alliance achieved yet another strategic communication goal: that of conveying a greater message, one of readiness and resilience in the face of extreme situations. It demonstrated openness to the public opinion and created a fertile context for the exchange of good practices and enforced cooperation with the civilian society.

In what concerns the rhetoric that surrounds the recent Russia-Ukraine conflict, NATO's rhetoric followed the same line of thought used at the beginning of the war, in 2014. According to informed public opinion, Russia's invasion of Ukraine, which started in February 2022, brought the members of the Alliance close together (Adler 2022). This is largely due to the rhetoric the Organization has used to glue and solidify cooperation within its ranks, of which "NATO's response to Russia's invasion of Ukraine" (October 2022) and the text of the Madrid Summit Declaration, issued a few months earlier (July 2022) are illustrations of effective language deployed in order to convey the ideology of cooperative power: "We welcome efforts of all Allies engaged in providing support to Ukraine" (Madrid Summit Declaration, par. 4). Paragraph 3 of the Declaration uses strong language that explicitly communicates the Alliance's criticism of the Russian invasion of Ukraine ("gravely undermines," "blatant violation," "cruelty"). There is also reference to Russia's "irresponsible rhetoric," a clear indication that NATO places great emphasis on the power of language and the effects of reckless discourse, and seriously condemns and intends to combat such destructive practices.

The selected examples emphasize the preoccupation of the military as an organization to invest efforts and institutional resources in converting communication into an active diplomatic dialogue, aimed at building bridges between the military and the civilian society and at reinforcing ideologies, values, and virtues that are specific to this field and that should function as models that other organizations might emulate.

By and large, a (for now) holistic glance at the modern military dis-course has yielded a rich crop of ideological landmarks that are overarching concepts such as globalization, security and defense, sustainable peace, co-operation, crisis management, and mitigation of armed conflicts. These, in addition to other elements of Euro-Atlantic geopolitics and strategy, influence and define military communication in the current global context and determine, at the same time, the salient ideological values inherent in the military discourse of the 21st century.

3 A proposed analytical framework for the CDA of military communication

The proposed framework channels theoretical and empirical practices of analysis toward the construction of a hybrid model of CDA, resulting from the triangulation of the three approaches detailed at the beginning of this chapter. The relevance of this study stems from analyzing military discourses which promote (new) values, beliefs, attitudes, and ideologies, which underpin and explicate the importance, role, and purpose of the military organization against the sociopolitical background of the events that generate them. The discovered salient features of the discourses have been further intertwined in the form of discourse strands, organized around a nexus of collective ideological stereotypes that were dissected from a diachronic perspective, with the aim of identifying the characteristics of simultaneous discourses, while paralleling their similarities and differences. The method proposed in this study synchronically and diachronically integrates Wodak's historical approach into Fairclough's three-dimensional analytical framework that marries text, talk, and discourse under the umbrella of the social practice. Complementary to these methods, the application of Van Dijk's analysis of macrostructures, formal structures, local meanings, local discourse forms, specific linguistic realizations, and context has dug even deeper into the layers of the military discourse, trying to identify the relevant elements defining the relationship between cognition and discourse. The findings of the investigation have been interpreted in terms of Van Dijk's sociocognitive theory of social representations, in an attempt to identify the concepts, ideas, attitudes, beliefs, and images that are prevalent in military discourse from the perspective of ideology, and which are relevant for locating specific instances illustrating the dynamics of power within the military organization.

Examining military discourse at word level includes identifying points of intersection between language, ideology, and power relations. CDA has proven to be the best suited method in the exploration of the construction of meaning of the social world. The current analysis of ideology has drawn upon the essential role of context and culture in discursive manifestations of military communication. The chosen analytical framework provides a different way of theorizing language and focuses on the investigation of discourses specific to sociocultural contexts (the military institution), while appealing to a method of data analysis that reveals the inner mechanisms that go into the discursive construction of communication.

The investigative paradigm proposed by this thesis is founded on the assumption that CDA is "the close study of language in use" (Taylor 2001:5), and that although its primary object of study is discourse, it may take excursions into many different connected fields (philosophy, psychology, sociology, anthropology). Loosely defined, an analysis of the discourse will look at "how stretches of language, considered in their full textual, social and psychological context become meaningful and unified for their users" (Cook 1989:ix). This idea was also developed in the works of J.R. Firth, the founder of modern British linguistics, who saw language not as an autonomous system but as part of a culture, which is in turn responsive to the environment. Hence, discourse analysis represents a theoretical frame of understanding the cultural environment and the phenomena associated with it as emerging in communication from the values and beliefs conveyed by means of language.

In the present study, the scrutinized cultural environment is the one pertaining to the military organization, and the discursive representations of communication characteristic to this community of practice are explored so as to identify the ideological values encompassed by the military discourse. Some key principles have emerged as relevant to the construction of an analytical framework by which to investigate military communication: the concept of intertextuality, the contextualized investigation of language use, and the analysis of ideology from a critical perspective.

3.1. Intertextuality

The concept of intertextuality is one of the central principles in discourse analysis. Julia Kristeva's coinage of the term represents an endeavor to fuse the semiotics of Ferdinand de Saussure with Mikail Bakhtin's (1981) "heteroglossia,"[22] or multiple meanings, i.e., the examination of the interrelatedness between language and discourses, by which "meaning is not transferred directly from writer to reader but instead is mediated through, or filtered by 'codes' imparted to the writer and reader by other texts" (Kristeva 1980:69). It is beyond doubt that military communication benefits from and even dwells on the concept of intertextuality, given that the weight and essence of the ideological concepts inherent in the discourse of the military largely depend on the background information characteristic to a specific social, political, or cultural context. The production and the meaning of language deployed in the articulation of the military communication are shaped by the experiences of those who produce the discourse (individuals and organizations alike). Bakhtin further argues that the deployment of meaning and language in discourse is controlled by social groups, institutions, organizations, and the relationships within them. As a consequence, the language of the military discourse is subject to manifold interpretations and conceptualizations based on sociocultural contexts or intentions. An analysis of the discursive materializations of military communication must contemplate the multitude of meanings that go beyond a single text in its unique interpretation. The concept of intertextuality lies at the foundation of any investigation that aims at interpreting the myriad of meanings inherent in any significant social discourse.

Starting from Leitch's definition according to which a "text is not an autonomous or unified object, but a set of relations with other texts" (qtd. in Porter 1986:35), intertextuality can also be described as a "web of meanings" (Vygotsky 1986:182). An intertextual investigation of language is actually a quest "for 'traces', the bits and pieces of Text which writers or speakers borrow and sew together to create new discourse" (Porter 1986:34). Rigorous examinations of texts assist researchers in conceptualizing texts as unified products of the historical and social context that generated them, and which inherently carry specific values, beliefs, attitudes, and, ultimately, ideologies.

In Fairclough's view, intertextuality is "the property texts have of being full of snatches of other texts, which may be explicitly demarcated or merged in, and which the texts may assimilate, contradict, ironically echo, and so forth" (1992:84). This definition accounts for the view that discourse strands are constantly recontextualized and reconceptualized so as to fit the social and discursive practices of the times they occur in. Consequently, the nub of the investigation central to this work is based on the premises that discourses are created, understood, and assimilated based on the historical, cultural, and social experiences of the social actors in a specific context.

Per Linell's approach on recontextualization delineates the notion as the "dynamic transfer-and-transformation of something from one discourse/text-in-context ... to another" (1998:154). Several scholars have noted that recontextualization is prone to significant ideological and political ramifications. For example, Adam Hodges (2008) dedicated his studies to the manner in which officials in the White House reconsidered and transformed a general's commentaries in a new political context, emphasizing the positive elements in the general's statements while softening the negative aspects. John Oddo (2014) also discovered that U.S. media reporting on Colin Powell's 2003 U.N. discourse reformed Powell's speech by recontextualizing it, conferring Powell's affirmations greater confidence and warrantability and even substantiated it with new proofs in support of the author's allegations. Oddo further argues that recontextualization is a future-oriented method of meaning manipulation, translated by another practice he identifies as "precontextualization." He defines it as "a form of anticipatory intertextuality wherein a text introduces and predicts elements of a symbolic event that is yet to unfold" (78). Translated into practice, this was visible in the way in which U.S. reporters predicted Powell's U.N. speech, drawing his future discourse into the normative present.

With these examples in mind, an analysis of military discourse must scrutinize a wider array of discourses and perceive texts as attributable to other meanings characteristic to the society and the culture in which the discourse is produced. Investigating military discourse should start from the premise that no text is original and exclusive and that, especially when the communication of ideologies is at stake, much if not the entire message is actually a rephrasing and a re-setting of old values in new contexts.

3.2. Language in context

Discourse analysis is concerned with investigating how speakers make use of the variability and unpredictability of language in order to iron into coherent versions of reality that are embedded in social, political, historical, and cultural contexts. Linguists argue that attitudes, beliefs, values, representations, and perceptions of people are variable depending on different contexts. Furthermore, they are fabricated in close dependability with historical, political, social, and cultural frameworks of discourse and interpersonal relations. Different people have different perceptions about a given phenomenon. In order to decode its meanings into comprehensible data, people utilize discursive devices at hand so as to negotiate, transfer, build, and represent their own interpretation of the phenomenon.

The analysis of language in a particular type of discourse explores the relationship between the producers of the discourse and their historical, social, and cultural background. The interpretation of a certain phenomenon, in terms of attitudes and reactions to it, may stem from a specific root in the background recognized as ideology, culture, or religion. From the analyst's perspective, this means that the contextual analysis of language is a quest for patterns and frameworks identifiable in the discursive environment. Such an assertion links back to the aforementioned theory of intertextuality which defines textual analysis in relation to a specific context or background.

As Stephanie Taylor (2001) remarks, one suitable methodology in discourse analysis is to look for language templates within larger contexts, i.e., discursive milieus incorporating "society" or "culture," an examination which views language as an important element of broader activities and processes in a given environment.

Language production and meaning making are significantly related to the repertoires which individuals or institutions make use of in decoding reality. These include values, beliefs, and diverse associated philosophies that characterize and define language use. William Stiles (2003) recognizes the uniqueness of all social events in that their interpretation is shaped by the participants' and observers' personal histories and the sequence of previous and subsequent episodes of making meaning out of experience. This view makes social discourse sequentially situated; the initial setting in which the discourse first occurs has major importance and contours what is being transmitted later on.

Traced back to the principle of intertextuality, the examination of language in context is essentially reduced to the practice of identifying representations of the world and constructed meanings. The negotiation of meaning making is a process of gluing together the society's perceptions about a given phenomenon, which obviously vary depending on the purpose, circumstance, and context of the discourse. Since the participants in a social interaction are, at the same time, the producers and the products of the culture and society they belong to, the validity of a phenomenon must be accordingly interpreted in terms of the specific social and cultural background.

Especially in the case of military communication, which is by definition a method of propaganda which transmits values and beliefs within and outside the organization, the discourse produced is construed as position-taking manifestations on a given political, social, and/or strategic phenomenon. In addition, the purpose of the discourse, in this particular case, is to either strategically repudiate certain aspects or validate criticism (Willig 2008; Potter and Wetherell 1987). These attitudes are definitely shaped by the contextualized sociocultural experiences generated by the communicative event.

In analyzing the structure of language use in context, discourse analysts can also be subjective in negotiating and representing different versions of social reality. Consequently, discourse analysts are dynamically concerned with the negotiation and production of meaning in order to produce valid representations of the investigated reality. More than merely reporting descriptions of stable and durable truth, the discourse researcher instinctively assigns meanings to discursive resources deployed in communication, without obliterating the context in which language occurs.

Nevertheless, the impact of discourse analysts in negotiating and constructing versions of reality is inescapably problematic to measure. Given that the investigator belongs to the social reality which hosts the research, they will inevitably contribute some of their personal experiences in dealing with the investigated topic. The concern about a discourse analyst's own assumptions and the possible impact these may have on the investigation itself is reasonable. To fight this bias, discourse researchers instinctively search for a pattern in the discourse, as it stems from a given context, and offer rigorous analyses based on values, norms, views, principles, ideals, and the social and cultural practices rooted in the communicative environment. CDA, by consequence, thoroughly obeys the principles of flexibility and reflexivity, as the historical, social, and cultural experiences of the researchers and of the entities under investigation outline and channel the interpretation and analysis of data. In essence, it is advisable that discourse researchers be self-aware of their own beliefs and presuppositions and that their interest and connection to the issue is not regarded "negatively as bias, but as a position to be acknowledged" (2003:17).

3.3. A critical approach to ideology

Van Dijk briefly synthesizes the multidisciplinary lens (social, cognitive, and discursive) through which ideological values should be explored:

> As "systems of ideas," ideologies are sociocognitively defined as social representations of social groups, and more specifically, as "axiomatic" principles of such representations. As the basis of the social group's self-image, ideologies organize its identity, actions, aims, norm and values and resources, as well as its relations to other social groups. (2006:115)

According to the same author, ideologies are manifested through the social practices of the group they define, and acquired, validated, altered, and disseminated through discourse. As a large group, or a broad organization, the military can be defined as a "community of practice" which possesses its own discursive patterns of communication and which uses language to absorb, confirm, change, and transmit the ideological values branding it. A critical analysis of the ideology deployed in the linguistic construction of the military discourse offers powerful instruments for the study of the structures and functions of fundamental ideologies. A sound ideological analysis of the discourse explicitly relates ideologies and language, in virtue of the many similarities they share.

From a sociocognitive perspective, "ideologies are defined as basic systems of fundamental social cognitions and organizing the attitudes and other social representations shared by members of groups" (Van Dijk 1995b:1). Language is also social because its functions are social. Ideologies are conceptualized as a mental representation comprising different elements such as "identity/membership, task, goal, norms, positions," all of which typify and model the values and beliefs shared by a group (1). Discourses are, in their turn, described as abstract systems of form, meaning, and interaction: lexical items, syntactic structures, connotation, and denotation, all of which cannot be observed directly but are subject to interpretation. They become abstract objects of investigation for language theory and, at the same time, are mental constructs of language. Consequently, meaning has a cognitive nature and any analysis of discourse automatically implies cognitive notions: knowledge, beliefs, opinions and ideologies.

"The point of ideological discourse analysis is not merely to 'discover' underlying ideologies, but to systematically link structures of discourse with structures of ideologies" (Van Dijk 1995a:143). In other words, a study of discourse, which is not based on a naïve knowledge of language, discourse, society, and ideology, but rather on analytically explicit methods, needs to dissolve any intuition we may have about the meaning of language and target explicitly what patterns of discourse generate specific inferences or mental deductions.

To this aim, Van Dijk proposes the following levels of CDA that connect ideologies and language from the sociocognitive perspective:

Level 1 – Social analysis, proposing an investigation of overall societal structures (e.g., parliamentary democracy, capitalism, dictatorship), institutional/organizational structures (e.g., political parties, government, the military), group relations (e.g., discrimination, hegemony), group structures (i.e., identity, task, goals, norm, position, resources).

Level 2 – Cognitive analysis, which espouses social cognition and personal cognition as secondary levels of analysis. Social cognition explores sociocultural values (e.g., solidarity, loyalty, ethos), ideologies (e.g., racist, sexist, feminist), systems of attitudes (e.g., multiculturalism), sociocultural knowledge (e.g., society, groups, individuals, language, culture). In its turn, personal cognition is divided into general/context-free cognition, referring to personal values (personal selections from the pool of social values), personal ideologies (personal interpretations of group ideologies), personal attitudes (systems of personal opinions) and personal knowledge (biographical information, past experiences) and particular/context-bound cognition, integrating models (ad hoc representations of specific current actions, events), context models (ad hoc representations of the speech context), mental plans and representations of acts and discourse, mental constructions of text meaning and mental selections of discourse structures (style).

Level 3 – Discourse analysis, examining various structures of text and talk. At this level, the investigation specifically targets the linguistic dimension of discourse: phonological (stress, pitch, volume, intonation) or graphical structures (headlines, bold characters, layout); syntactic structures (word order, topicalization, clausal relations, split constructions); semantic structures (explicit vs. implicit, implications – insinuations, vagueness, presuppositions, allusions, symbolism, collective symbolism, figurativeness, metaphorism); pragmatics (intention, mood, opinion, perspective, relative distance); formal structures (idioms, sayings, clichés, set phrases, language patterns); logic and composition of the discourse (argumentation – strategy, types, cohesion, coherence). (1995a:20)

In line with Van Dijk's framework, military discourse has been studied from these three perspectives so as to identify the way in which ideologies are constructed, embedded, and conveyed through language. The final aim is to pinpoint the specific instances and events in which the discourse of power is fixed and to describe, explain, and interpret the way in which the dynamics of power relations are operationalized through language. The starting point has been an overall analysis of the military as an organization, followed by a cognitive exploration of the sociocultural values and ideologies embedded in and conveyed by military discourse, while the final step entails a thorough study of various structures of text, dissected from a linguistic perspective.

In essence, both language and discourse enjoy a wide array of formational possibilities to conceptualize ideological representations that shape the shared sets of beliefs and values of the society. In relation to ideologies, the structures of discourse hold a dual functionality: to enact the essential values and beliefs and to act as an instrument of persuasion, influencing preferred mental models and, ultimately, favored attitudes and ideologies. It is in this latter way, Van Dijk concludes, that "the formation, change and challenge of ideologies are a function of discourse structure" (1995c:146).

This chapter has delineated the main operational elements of CDA as a method of qualitative investigation, with a focus on the key terms employed in the deconstruction and interpretation of military discourse (criticality, text, and context). Against this background, an analytical framework has been identified, and the empirical application will be based on three main pillars supporting this investigative paradigm (intertextuality, the examination of language in context, and a critical perspective of ideology). Military discourse will be investigated through the sociocognitive prism proposed by Van Dijk, which reunites three different layers of analysis to describe the discursive manifestations that occur at the intersection between language, ideology, and the notion of power. The proposed analysis will also integrate Wodak's historical approach, centered on a two-directional timeline that will scrutinize military discourse both synchronically and diachronically. Fairclough's three-dimensional analytical framework that espouses text, talk, and discourse under the umbrella of the social practice will also be employed so as to offer a substantiation of the notion that military discourse is a manifestation of institutional practices associated with and promoted by the military organization. The main object of investigation, i.e., military discourse, has also been broadly conceptualized and given a definition located at the convergence point between sociology, psychology, and linguistics, against the backdrop of an outer perspective dictated by the current geo-political, geo-strategic, cultural, and social challenges that shape and define the discourse of the present military organization.

In sum, CDA is the most suitable method for the investigation of military discourse – and any type of discourse, for that matter – due to a wide range of reasons: it is based on an interdisciplinary approach, which is extremely relevant when interpreting a type of discourse situated at the intersection between historical, social, political, and military contexts; it offers an eclectic combination between different theories and methodologies and provides not only a description and an interpretation of the object under investigation but also an explanation thereof; the approach taken is problem-oriented rather than focused on specific linguistic items; categories and tools for analysis are defined in accordance with the specific problem under investigation; it offers an addictive approach which entails a continual movement back and forth between theory and empirical data; the historical, social, and political context is also examined and integrated into the interpretation of discourses.

4 Ideology, discourse, and power

The main objective of this chapter is to conceptualize the most important elements of the nexus that encapsulates and relates ideology, power, and discourse. The theory of ideology put forward here is articulated based on a theoretical framework connecting discourse and power, represented as elements of the same social construct. Approached from a tripartite perspective, the notion of "ideology" is interpreted from cognitive, social, and discursive angles, a triangulation that converges toward a multidisciplinary delineation of the term.[3] The overarching theorization of ideology is narrowed down and funneled toward its manifestations at the level of NATO discourse. To this aim, this section of the book examines the link between NATO ideology and discourse, with particular focus on the manner in which the Alliance's doctrine has been operationalized in the language of the most important NATO documents.

The chapter also places a great deal of emphasis on different dimensions of power, as historically defined in specialized literature, and achieves an informed transition from the general ideology of power to specific representations of power in NATO discourse. The different concepts of power are located at the intersection between military ideology and discourse, with particular focus on those particular types of power whose manifestations are illustrative for the dynamics influencing and generating either the cohesion or the division of the North Atlantic Organization.

4.1. Defining ideology

From a cognitive viewpoint, ideology is described as the multitude of diverse social perceptions and interpretations of reality shared by the members of the group. Cognition explains the mental dimension of ideologies, their manifestation as ideas, beliefs, norms, values, the dialectical

---

3   A theoretical approach to the critical analysis of ideologically driven discourses has been published as an article in the Journal of Romanian Literary Studies, 11/2017, pp. 309–402, E-ISSN 2248-3004, under the title *A Theoretical Framework for the Critical Analysis of Ideologically-Driven Discourses.*

relation between opinion and knowledge, and their status as shared representations of reality. The social facet defines the characteristics of the individuals, groups, or institutions implicated in the development and reproduction of ideologies and sheds further light on the types of relations existing between the members of these groups. The discursive dimension explains how daily text and talk, verbal interaction, and communication at large are influenced by ideologies, and how discourse is conceived as a linguistic materialization of ideologies and used as an instrument of ideological dissemination of knowledge in society.

In embarking on a journey of investigating the manner in which ideologies are ironed into coherent discourse, one must start from the premise that discourse is the linguistic vehicle through which ideologies are expressed, construed, and legitimized. Since the end of the 18th century, when French philosopher Destutt de Tracy devised the term, the notion of "ideology" has received a myriad of definitions, forged and adapted to suit a number of different – and often divergent – domains of study, including mass media (Said 1981; Schmid 1982), politics (Rosenberg 1988), and social sciences (Larrain 1979; Abercombie 1980; Thompson 1990; Eagleton 1991; Fairclough 2001). Although de Tracy defined ideology as "the science of ideas," this slightly restricted approach to interpreting and analyzing what we think, speak, and argue has been long appreciated as obsolete, and modernist and postmodernist scholars have enlarged the scope of ideology, defining it as "a system of beliefs" (Van Dijk 1995a:18), false consciousness (Engels's interpretation of Marxism), social cognition (Fiske and Taylor 1991; Chomsky 1993), mental and social representations (Johnson-Laird 1983; Farr and Moscovici 1984; Garnham 1987), and ultimately simply as norms and values organizing individuals, groups, and institutions.

Starting from the assumption that ideologies are neither private nor personal, since they are socially shared in collectivity, ideologies can be further defined as social interpretations that define the social distinctiveness of a group, united by a system of commonly accepted values and norms embraced as fundamental and axiomatic, aimed at controlling and organizing the existence and the image of the organization. In this respect, one of the major functions of ideologies is to provide consistency to the philosophies of a social group and promote a common background for their acquisition and use in daily contexts. More importantly, ideologies also stipulate which cultural ideals (viz., justice, freedom, democracy, etc.) are relevant for the organization and define their role and importance for the cohesion of the institution. Observably, within an organization, such as the military, ideologies are legislated by action and interaction, and their reproduction is deeply rooted in institutional practices.

If interpreted as sociocognitive representations of the (rapidly changing) world, ideologies are most often acquired gradually and sometimes modified over time. It takes many experiences and many discursive materializations thereof in order to acquire an ideology; the same is true for when ideologies are changed. In the words of Van Dijk, "the often-observed variability of ideological opinions of group members ... should be accounted for at the personal or contextual level" (2006:117). Consequently, the rejection of a stable group ideology must not be done depending on individual responses to life experiences.

4.2. The social-cognitive function of ideology

The proposed theoretical approach to ideology is much in line with other contemporary methodologies targeting a definition of the notion. Rosenberg, Thompson, or Eagleton also view ideologies as a "system of ideas" attributing them both social and cognitive dimensions. Localized between societal organizations and configurations of the mind, ideologies are seen as basic frameworks of social cognition, having precise internal structures as well as social and cognitive roles. Flanked by cognitive representative images and processes essential for the materialization of speech and action, on one hand, and socially situated positions and goals of social communities, on the other, ideologies often aim to validate command and authority, to articulate opposition in relationships of power, or to promote basic guidelines for the behavior of professional categories (scientists, journalists, doctors, teachers) and institutions (hospitals, schools, the military).

The sociocultural knowledge shared by the members of a group is an essential segment of the social system, as individuals are affiliated to the group in virtue of their common beliefs, values, and opinions, systematized into social behavior. In this context, ideologies are constructed as abstract mental and social schemes that organize socially shared attitudes.

They are gradually acquired by the members of the group through processes of socialization and, once internalized, they regulate and control the
social manifestation of the group as assumed social practice.

Socially, ideologies incorporate the elementary collective features of
the group, are such as tasks, goals, objectives, values, norms, position,
identity, and resources. Contemporary militarist ideologies, for instance,
represent modern warfare in terms of conflictual situations between the
"good" and the "bad," between the Western world and the terrorists, a
context in which the identity, values, and resources of the free world are
"threatened" by the others. The discursive materialization of this antagonism is located in the linguistic separation between "us" and "them," a
distinction further exploited by the opposition of positive and negative
properties and actions associated to the two divergent parties. The group's
ideology is built on a mutually agreed upon selection of relevant social
principles, as both the organization as a whole and its individuals attach
extraordinary importance to values such as independence, freedom, democracy, peace, and equality. Theoutgroup, on the other hand, is defined
by beliefs like self-identity, extremism, and radicalism, an ideology labeled
as malignant, "characterized by contempt for human dignity and freedom
and a depraved disregard for human life" (Chertoff 2008:11). This identity
dimension of the group is visible in the schematic organization of the ideology, reflected in the collective mind and shared by members as assumed
property of the group within societal structures. It also organizes knowledge, information, and actions at institutional level and is of paramount
importance in defining the conditions of affiliation and membership. Ideological landmarks further define the position of the group in reference to
other groups, identified as "terrorists," "extremists," "radicalists," etc.
In a nutshell, I may assert that the basic social functions of ideologies en-
able members of a group to establish (admission to) their group, to define
its identity and regulate affiliation processes, and to organize their social
objectives and the actions directed toward their accomplishment.

Perceived through the lens of social cognition, ideologies cogently entail
cognitive functions. In addition to organizing, monitoring, and controlling
the group's attitudes and behavior, ideologies also regulate the organization, the development, and the application of sociocultural knowledge.
Located at the intersection between the social and the individual, ideologies

and the knowledge controlled by them influence the personal cognition of the members of the group, translating personal experiences and the mental representations associated to them into "models" of social practice (Van Dijk and Kintsch 1983:72). Defined as mental representations of events, actions, and situations people experience, these models represent the personal and unique knowledge and opinions stemming from the biographical practice of the individuals. Nonetheless, these experiences are socially controlled and intertwined in a nexus of collective social cognitions shared within the group, which makes them part of a combined personal and instantiated social information materialized into mental models. Their application to the interpretation of reality is essential in making explicit the relation between group ideologies and discourse. In sum, the cognitive dimension of ideology explains how the shared mental models of social representations control text and talk and how individuals understand, interpret, and apply the social practices specific to the group they belong to.

By and large, ideologies are shaped and defined by a set of social and cognitive functions. They consolidate and fundament the social representations the members of an ideological group share. They constitute the most substantiated origin of discourse and generate the social practices through which group members validate their affiliation and membership. Allowing group participants to coordinate and manage their actions and interactions toward accomplishing the ultimate goals of the organization, ideologies act as catalysts in channeling the joint efforts of the individuals on their path to becoming an entity adhering to the same values and principles. Lastly, ideologies act as the missing link between social structures and their discourses and actions, thus filling the void separating the cognitive and the social dimensions of individual representations of the world and forging them into durable collective models.

4.3. Structures of ideology and structures of discourse

As an investigative entry point, ideological discourse analysis is concerned with discovering the ideologies inherent in discourse and, more importantly, with systematically connecting structures of ideology with structures of discourse. In order to explain the structure and properties of ideologies, Van Dijk has hypothesized a general ideological schema and postulates that "in order to be acquired and used, ideologies need some kind of organization" (2006:118). This assertion leads us to the idea that ideologies are not extensive, unordered, chaotic sets of beliefs but are systematized according to a pattern, and have a structural organization. Since ideologies are complex cognitive representations, they are organized around a series of predictable categories allowing social actors to recognize, comprehend, construct, alter, or even discard different beliefs. The categories that enter in the composition of the ideological schemata are derivative from the inherent characteristics of the social group and regulate the identity as well as the identification of the members to the group. The same author has identified six categories reflecting the levels that compose the structure of ideologies: membership criteria, typical activities, overall aims, norms and values, position, resources (Van Dijk 2006). These categories control and govern individual and collective actions and also mentally organize the representative models of ideology. Consequently, social groups can be defined in terms of identity and membership, specific actions, goals, and beliefs.

This purely theoretical schemata become plausible if applied to practical research and used to explain social practices, such as discourse. If ideologies, as assumed above, are structured on the basis of a schematic representation, then it is only expected to infer that discourses are also structured under the influence of the specific ideologies they enact. Weiss and Wodak (2007) argue that discursive practices are, at the same time, structured and structuring actions, i.e., they organize ideologies and are, conversely, organized by them.

The assertion that discourse is socially and cognitively structured starts from the premise that ideologies are the core of social judgments, expressed through ideologically controlled propositions, in the form of assumptions, opinion, viewpoints, and evaluations of reality. Looking at discourse as a structured social practice allows its interpretation and analysis from the perspective of social structures, social action, and the agency associated to it (Fairclough 2003).

An analytically explicit examination of discourse needs to specify expressions and meanings embedded in linguistic materializations and closely investigate the mental representations displayed in communication. In discourse, ideologies are typically expressed in units of meaning, linguistically defined as clauses, symbolized as networks of conceptual nodes organizing mental representations of the world. They imply a certain syntax (topicalization, word order, clausal relations: fronted vs. embedded, main vs. subordinate), specific semantic structures (explicit vs. implicit, lexical polarizations, codes), rhetorical devices (repetitions, euphemisms, litotes), and pragmatic aspects (self-congratulation vs. allegation, declaration vs. rejection, boasting vs. derogation). In short, discourses and the language deployed in the production thereof benefit from a wide array of structural mechanisms used to express ideologically controlled opinions. Discourse structures are connected to the structure of ideologies in that they enact the fundamental ideologies and promote favored mental models, attitudes, and values.

A diversity of discursive strategies and structures are deployed in expressing ideological beliefs as well as the consequent personal and social opinions. They allow the discovery of linkages between ideologies and discourse at a structural level. Ideological discourses, by extension, will characteristically be semantically concerned with specific themes, local meanings, and implications in providing descriptions of: self-identity – membership, affiliation, origin, properties, history, boundaries; activities – tasks, activities, expectations, social roles; goals – objectives usually labeled as ideologically situated positive actions that are not necessarily factual (e.g., ensuring peace and stability, defending the interests of the country/alliance, peace-building, etc.); norms and values – oppositions of good / bad, right / wrong, truth / lie, equality / inequality, tolerance / intolerance, democracy / oppression, etc.; position and relations – group relations, conflict, power dynamics, polarization; resources – information, knowledge, expertise, etc.

4.4. Ideology and discourse processing

The identification and deconstruction of the specific ideologies deployed in discourse can be operationalized by interpreting discourses from a linguistic and sociocognitive perceptive, based on an articulated conceptual framework that connects knowledge, cognitive models, and context. The processes involved in decomposing the explicit or often hidden meaning of communication start from the premise that ideologies are the foundation of discourse. Processing discourse actually summarize as processing ideologies, since the values, norms, and beliefs of a group are acquired and expressed by spoken and written communicative instances and inter-action. When the members of a group (institution, organization) legitimate their actions, they linguistically materialize them in the form of ideologi-cally driven discourses.

Most investigations of discourse processing focus on understanding the social practices, and, implicitly, the discourses that make the ideologies be observable, i.e., clearly verbalized and articulated. In spite of the ample literature on ideology, there are basically few critiques that explicitly in-vestigate and explain the relations between ideology and discourse. None-theless, there are sufficient CDA monographs which tackle at least some aspects of this connection (Pêcheux 1982; Wodak et al. 1987; Wodak 1989; Fairclough 2001; Wodak and Meyer 2009).

As discussed in the previous section, the link between discourse and ideology is established on the basis of structures of discourse: syntactic structures (agency), polarized lexical items (*us* and *them*), implications, metaphors, argumentation, and other discourse characteristics. However, Alessandro Duranti and Charles Goodwin (1992) argue that it does not suffice to merely witness ideologically based linguistic devices used in the construction of discourses, but that it is critical to theorize discourse pro-cessing in terms of context structures. Contexts are actually the interface between the social situation and the communicative event, cognitively conceptualized as mental models, i.e., as specific representations through which social actors experience, understand, and represent the significant aspects of the circumstances they are part of. These mental models facilitate the connection between the discourse and the social/political/cultural con-text in which it is produced, in terms of subject (who), topic (what about), location (where), time (when), audience (to whom), etc. Such features are relevant for the comprehension of the communicative situation and con-trol a wide range of discourse processing stages, while validating the so-cial appropriateness of the discourse. Defined as "subjective participant definitions of communicative situations" (Van Dijk 2004:735), contexts may be ideologically biased, thus resulting in subjective discourses (e.g., discourses that have a more or less respectful tone or lexical choices).

Contexts are equally instrumental in the processes of construction and reception of discourses, since the information inherent in the context model (from a pragmatic perspective, for instance, in terms of the "who is involved") controls the speech acts of the communicative event. One utterance can be, at the same time, perceived as a promise or as a menace, depending on the power dynamics regulating the relationship between the social actors, their position within the organization, their (expressed or hidden) intentions, etc. In the same manner, semantic context models contextualize and control the selection of information, the choice of the topic, and the type of the information to be transmitted. Furthermore, context models regulate the style of the discourse, i.e., all grammatical choices (pronominalization, syntax) that define the situation, translated in the selection of the various levels of formality or registers specifically tailored to the circumstances. The format of the discourse is also influenced by these models, which ultimately control the mechanics of communication in terms of organization, structure, layout, etc.

While mental contexts are personal and characterized by a high degree of subjectivity, the ideologies, attitudes, and knowledge shared by the members of a group are more general and claim an uncontested status of legitimacy. As an essential instrument in controlling the production and the reception of discourses, knowledge is learnt and normally presupposed by the majority of the individuals belonging to different communities (culture, city, nation, organization). This commonly accepted, taken-for-granted information makes it possible for discourse meanings to be decoded and interpreted on a mutual ground by the members of the same community. Since it is essentially defined as socially shared beliefs, knowledge is also ideological and consequently contributory to the production of mental models and of the discourses founded on them. It acquires an over-arching dimension and receives a definition at the level of the social group, and not of the individual.

Interpreted at macro level, knowledge becomes an idealization, a conceptual abstractization shared by a community, whose members, however, do not conceptualize it similarly. Within a community, knowledge is differentiated or stratified, according to the different degrees of expertise and education of the members of the group. Against this background, discourse processing is actually an analysis of the tip of the iceberg, the location where non-presupposed meanings are partially explicated. For the purpose of our ideological investigation of discourse, we will refer to an average base level of knowledge, commonly understood by all members of the community, and will define it as shared beliefs that are presumed in public discourses and openly addressed to the community.

4.5. Ideologies as vehicles of power

The previous section has provided an overview of the functions of ideologies and the social and cognitive aspects that lie on at the basis of an argumentation legitimizing the need for ideologies. At micro-level, i.e., at the level of the individuals that compose a group, ideologies are instrumental in organizing the social representations, in controlling the social practices and the discourse associated to them, and finally in facilitating action and interaction between the ingroup members and their cooperation with individuals located outside the group. At macro-level, however, ideologies are more concerned with regulating the relations existing within a group, and in this sense directed at legitimizing relations of power, among other ideological landmarks.

Traditionally, ideologies have been constantly defined as instruments validating the dominance by various organizations or elite groups. They endorse the practices of the prevailing group members, conceptualizing the principles that justify, certify, condone, or acknowledge various forms of power. Defined as the mental embodiment of the notion and practice of "control," ideologies are basically the vehicles of materialization of social power into action. Since discourses are often defined as a form of action, it can be inferred that ideologically construed discursive materializations are the legitimate locus of the enactment of control, through the very properties and structures of discourse: context, topic, style, etc.

The relation between ideology and discourse from a cognitive and social perspective has already been discussed. Against this background and acknowledging the role of ideologies in constructing mental models of representation and comprehension of reality, the discussion continues with the inclusion of the concept of power under the umbrella of ideologies from an entry point located at the intersection between discourse, control, and the mind. Starting from the assumption that ideologies are embedded and vehiculated in discourse, controlling public discourse ultimately comprises guiding people's minds and inherently the ideologies and the social practices associated with them. The main interest of a critical view on ideologically driven discourses is essentially the manifestation of dominance and the role of ideologies in legitimizing power relations within a group.

There have been many schools of thought and scholars concerned with devising theories about the linkage between power and ideology. Marxist theories described ideologies in terms of the processes through which "the dominant ideas within a given society reflect the interest of a ruling economic class" (Stoddart 2007:192). Post-structuralist thinkers attribute language a social power and view discourse as the central milieu for the display of social philosophies and principles, and define the social space (social categories, institutions, organizations) as being eminently discursive (Derrida 1967; Foucault 1980; Torfing 1999). In line with Marxist models of ideologies, Frankfurt School theorists (Theodor Adorno, Walter Benjamin, Max Horkheimer. Herbert Marcuse) agree that social power functions throughout the cultural dimension of a society, but their view on the manifestations of ideology is somewhat limited, since in their assessment, the social function of ideological structures is to assimilate people into webs of domination and subordination. This is too ample an abstractization that divorces ideology and its discursive manifestation from the interactions occurring in everyday life. At the beginning of the 20th century, the unitary vision of Antonio Gramsci added greater complexity to the concept of ideology, subsequently funneled down to the notion of "hegemony," embedded in the author's dissimilarity between "coercion and consent as alternative mechanisms of social power" (Gramsci 1992:137). In contrast to the punishing role of violence and threat, hegemonic power is viewed as a practice of social power that relies on participation and voluntarism and which is directed to convincing individuals and groups to adhere to the ideology (i.e., social values and norms) of a fundamentally unequal system. By definition, this form of social power is hegemonic in that it is "inherited from the past and uncritically absorbed" and produced and disseminated with the help of civil society institutions (school, church, media) (Gramsci 1992, SNP: 333).

In Gramscian analysis, power inherently resides in ideology. I postulate that this theory explicitly applies to the military organization, seen as the locus of the legitimate manifestation of hegemonic power. As essential elements of the ideology specific to the military as a community of practice, power relations and power dynamics are inherited in virtue of the organizational culture, as an unchallenged status-quo which identifies the military institution and are non-judgmentally absorbed by means of informal and formal education (military high schools, academies, workplace environment, society, mass media, family). Moreover, the military environment is primarily characterized by the exercise of power, often materialized in the form of "war of position," a relational mechanism whose dynamics recycle and crystallize the pyramid of power, as subaltern groups or individual members realize their own capacity to advance toward higher levels of the hierarchy and accede to superior echelons, a constant movement that motivates them to maintain an active involvement in their profession and to promote inter group relations at all levels and in all directions of the chain of command.

The model that governs the relationship between power and ideology as applied to the military organization may also be perceived as a legitimate reinterpretation of Foucault's own assertions about power:

> Power must be analyzed as something which circulates, or rather as something which only functions in the form of a chain. It is never localized here and there, never in anybody's hands, never appropriated as a commodity or piece of wealth. Power is employed and exercised through a net-like organization. And not only do individuals circulate between its threads; they are always in the position of simultaneously undergoing and exercising this power. (1980: 96)

Another essentially critical aspect of Foucault's analysis of power is represented by his interest in deconstructing the reasons of power manifestation and objectifying power relations in the form of "anti-authority" struggles. He is concerned with "bringing to light power relations, locating their position, finding out point of applications and methods used" (Foucault 1982:783). In opposition to Louis Althusser's all-encompassing perception of human nature which defines man as "a perpetual subject of ideological construct" (qtd. in Daldal 2014:161), Foucault intends to decipher the methods by which the individual is turned into a subject in virtue of power relations. He identifies this theory as the "ideology-subject" model.

This form of power applies itself to immediate everyday life which categorizes the individual, marks him by his own individuality, attaches him to his own identity, imposes a law of truth on him which he must recognize, and which others have to recognize in him. It is a form of power which makes in individuals subjects. (1982:784)

The same author establishes three types of struggle – against subjection, domination, and exploitation. All three are embodied in the State, which is, in his interpretation, the central source of power. His theory is illustrative of the present investigation of power relations expressed in military discourse as a consequence of perceiving the State as the symbol of repressive apparatuses: Army, police, penal institutions. Against this backdrop, and following Foucault's own line of thought, the military acquires the proportion of a state institution whose ideological role is to diffuse power and create regimes of truth.

Rejecting the limited assertion that power is an institution in itself, both Foucault and Gramsci are united in the belief that power is a manifestation of force that can simply be materialized in action. Since the military is an action-oriented organization by excellence, I argue that, in this ideological context, power relations are characterized by a series of basic elements. First of all, power is seized, acquired, and shared, and also exercised from a wide range of positions and perspectives. Second, power manifests according to a schema of binary antagonism, opposing the rulers and the ruled, the leaders and the led. Lastly, power relations have a pre-defined objective, which makes them deliberate and intentional.

Whether seen as a product of ideology or as a system of relations generating knowledge, power is a complex notion that cannot be limited to a single perspective definition, but whose implications and applications to the study of discourse and ideology require an interdisciplinary approach. Suffice it to say, at this point, and for the sake of the undertaken investigation, that social power is representative for defining the relations between elements of diverse social formations and is manifested in discourse as a form of enacting and validating ideologies. Power is highly dependent on control over cognitive conditions and is exercised in the minds of the individuals, typically through discursive materializations such as persuasive or manipulative speech acts. A linguistic analysis of ideologically driven discourses is relevant only from the perspective of investigating to what extent power is exercised, legitimized, and maintained through language as a vehicle of social expression. In addition to direct communication involving speech acts such as requests, commands, and orders, the knowledge component required to apply and sustain power relations also relies on the existence of collective cultural beliefs, norms, and values, against the background of shared (or challenged) ideologies. This commonly accepted ideological framework is assimilated, validated, and reformed through discourse. In sum, the concept of ideology is fundamental when undertaking an investigation aimed at establishing the role of discourse in the enactment and validation of power.

4.6. Frameworks of power

Anyone reading the vast existing literature on power is bound to be troubled by the absence of a generally accepted definition of the concept. There have been numerous attempts by various authors to provide either unpretentious or comprehensive theories of power and, unfortunately, the differences are not merely semantic, which makes a construction of an overarching definition of power even more painstaking.

For the military organization of the present, the notion of power has always been the buzzword that has kept the institution coherent, and its individual elements linked under the umbrella of common objectives and shared values. No other definition of power as related to the context of the military, seen a collective entity, seems to be more illustrative than Talcott Parsons's. His elaboration of the concept of power links it to authority, consent, and a collective pursuit of common goals. According to Parson's explanation, power "is generalized capacity to secure the performance of binding obligations by units in a system of collective organization when the obligations are legitimized with reference to their bearing on collective goals" (1963:237). Power therefore is linked to the institutionalization of authority and "conceived as a generalized medium of mobilizing commitments or obligation for effective collective action" (Parson 1963:250). Following the same line of thought, Hannah Arendt considers power as an ability of the humans to act in concert: "Power is never the property of the individual; it belongs to a group and remains in existence only so long as the group keeps together" (1970:44). A correlation of these definitions results in the identification of several theoretical frameworks of power that have nonetheless been conceptualized numerous times under various forms in the existing literature dealing with theories of power. The most prevalent relate the concept of power to the notions of authority, collective agency, structure, and legitimacy.

As early as 1947, Weber's *A Theory of Social and Economic Organization* approaches power in direct relation to the concepts of authority and rule, defining it as a factor of domination, legitimately activated by formal authority. Although Weber's definition is rooted in his interests related to the mechanisms of bureaucracy and organizational thinking, it might be easily inserted within a military framework, especially when the institution of the armed forces is perceived in its formal authoritative dimension. Weber's discussion of organizational power is continued by Dahl (1961), who locates the concept of power inside the delimitations of a community. In the context of our theorization of power, the military can be seen as one of the most coherent social communities, defined as "a single unit, ordered according to a uniform principle, possessing a continuity of time and place, from which the power stems" (Sadan 1997:34). Such a centralized conceptualization of power comes in direct opposition to Foucault's post-structuralist approach, which refuses to acknowledge the existence of an ordered and regulating agency, dissolves fixed points of reference, and considers power to stem from a series of practices, rather than from structured actions. We would agree with Foucault's thinking only in that institutional practices could constitute a legitimate locus of power, with the mention that such practices cannot be divorced from the rational agency that endorses them.

Steven Lukes offers an explicit formulation of the relation between power and structure, which indelibly ties the notion of power to human agency. He notes: "Power presupposes human agency. To use the vocabulary of power (and its cognates) in application to social relationships is to speak of human agents separately or together, in groups or organizations, through actions or inactions, significantly affecting the thoughts or actions of others" (qtd. in Clegg 1997:100).

The military is a collection of human agents, organized according to a specific structure, whose actions (or inactions, as Lukes puts it) definitely impact on the actors involved in the social context where power, authority, control, and influence are some of the leveraging elements underpinning the dynamics of inter- and intra-relations and, implicitly, of institutional communication.

Any discussion that acknowledges the importance of social actors and recognizes the different varieties of relationships that configure their interaction must also envisage the importance of the dialectical connection between agency and structure. Drawing on Giddens's duality of structure, I can put forward a structuration theory of power as related to the military institution, where the concept of power is central to a circuit involving agency (individual actors or entities), rules (regulated interactions between actors, founded on values, principles, and ideologies), and resources. Within this model, power is essentially a structural concept, which organizes the central aspects of the functioning arrangement of any social system. The military is no exception. The structural properties of power are typically reified as the crystallization, institutionalization, or stabilization of interaction patterns. Power becomes an interactive process which defines the dynamics of the relations established between the actors involved in the organization and, at the same time, functions as one of its structural attributes.

The view of power as a mode of interaction unquestionably encompasses agency, rules, and resources. Against the setting of the current investigation that situates the concept of power within the notional boundaries of the military as an organization, some clarifications of this structural triangle must be brought.

First and foremost, agency in the military is the legitimate entity that acts as a stabilizer of power across a specific field of action. It is fundamentally contingent upon the subordination of the constitutive individual parts. The variable achievement of this subordination is regularly marked by the implication of power with the dialectic of resistance, stemming from the realistic view that power unavoidably involves mutual exchange "because it is always constituted within a relational universe of meaning" (Clegg 1989:189). One document that locates the agency dimension assumed by NATO is the *Nuclear Planning Group (NPG) Study #46*, published in 1974, after the NPG Ministers, assembled in Ankara 1973, had tasked the Permanent Representatives of the NPG with the initiation of a study on the implications of communicating NATO's intentions to the enemy, to other countries, and to the public. The document created the framework which gives NATO the possibility – and not the obligation – to communicate its intention of using nuclear weapons before actually engaging in it. The essential issues identified in the study are indicative of NATO's commitment to act as a legitimate power which assumes the agency of communicating its intentions to the other actors involved in a nuclear scenario.

In the classical Webberian sense, the whole concept of power and its subordinator value directs the analysis toward a taproot reaching back into the notion of discipline and hierarchy, two fundamental pillars that regulate organizational structure. Materializations of institutionalized forms of power are reinforced by a number of laws, regulations, and circulars, that control and manage all actions and behavior of the military, and anchor command in terms of rank and authority, allowing it to flow vertically between different reference groups (those to which one would like to belong, and to which one is identified) within the hierarchy. Perceived from the standpoint of the resources involved in its materialization, power manifests as a form of social control based on relevant socially valued yet unequally distributed resources, such as status, position, rank, authority, expertise, or affiliation to a dominant group. Discipline and hierarchical structure are indispensable to the armed forces institution because they allow an immediate recognition of the agency – holder of power. The military hierarchical organization is founded on the principle that, whatever the situation, in the presence of two members of the institution, one is necessarily subordinated to the other in virtue of their ranks and in order of seniority.[4] This ensures the official acknowledgment of the agent who is the holder of power, and who exercises power in an individualized and exclusive manner. Formally, through discipline (and the rules underlying it), the mode of devolution and the conditions for the exercise of power are

---

4   The meaning of duty, responsibility, and authority and the manner in which these concepts apply to every soldier in the military institution are defined and regulated in a series of military documents, usually Field Manuals (FM) or Army Regulations (AR), of which we selectively mention: FM 7-21-13/Chapter 3/Duties, Responsibilities and Authority of the Soldier; FM 6-0/Command and Control; FM 6-22 (22–100)/Army Leadership; FM 7-22.7/The Army Non Commissioned Officer Guide; AR 600-200/Army Command Policy.

determined. This model is actually observed in all bureaucratic institutions but with a particular force within the military institution. It makes the competition for power impossible between the social actors. Above all, it guarantees that, whatever the situation, orders will be given by a single source ~~that~~ and will be incontestable and executed. The hierarchical structure ensures unity and permanence of command in all circumstances. The purpose of the discipline is to restrict the autonomy of the performer to the mere application of orders. In this way, a rationalization of the social relations within the institution is carried out, agency is regulated and centralized, and situations in which the action of the army is fragmented and therefore ineffective and dangerous are avoided.

David Calleo (1987) has argued that, in assuming NATO leadership, the United States established a hierarchy in NATO and a global *Pax Americana* with NATO at its centerpiece. In forging transatlantic security, the assumed task of the United States was to ensure European security, by assisting the long-term effort of the Europeans to build a coherent identity framework that would be allied to and receptive to American leadership. The hierarchical power attributed to the United States in the context of this endeavor was materialized by the presence of American troops on the territory on Western Europe, tasked with the mission of defending this area against the Soviet threat. The United States was also to provide economic and military aid that would create enduring democratic political systems supported by a strong Western European defense. It basically meant that the Unites States would be the counter-power to balance Soviet power while Western Europe recuperated from its war-inflicted losses.

Second, power is implicated in authority and constituted by rules. Behavior in an organization is largely rule guided. However, rules are not absolute but rather open to diverse interpretations, and, unfortunately, not all interpretations are equal. Therefore, the reception, interpretation, and application of rules must be disciplined. This does not only refer to linguistic interpretations of different forms of military communication (as rules are typically fixed in written or, more rarely, spoken discourse). It traces back to the assimilation of organizational values and related behavior that needs to be regulated by discipline. Against this backdrop, military discipline becomes the conceptual and functional locus of legitimized power. Foucault's (1982) notion of disciplinary power is pertinent in this context so as to subsidize discipline as a mechanism of power which controls the conduct of people in society. The French philosopher argues that discipline is not conceptually equal to power, but that it can be rather defined as a way in which power can be exercised. From his perspective, proper functioning of the military institution is an expression of a power-induced positive outcome. In a similar vein, Wright Mills (1956) argues that the military enforces discipline in order to regulate and normalize the perception of the members of the military as a collectivity.

Moreover, the transformation of the existing rules or the production of new rules in the military organization is based on the idea that soldiers are supposed to experience a feeling of pride and honor through their obedience to the chain of command and therefore not challenge the values they have agreed to embrace, but rather accept them, according to the principles of compliance to orders and respect for hierarchy. In this context, discipline can be defined as the system which organizes the relations of power within the social group formed by the armed forces. It makes it possible to imprint rationality and formalization in the social relations synonymous with efficiency and cohesion. Discipline operates as a direct mechanism of behavioral control, by indirectly controlling what is acceptable and important to the institution. Ultimately, discipline is instrumental in emphasizing the differentiation and the creation (or rather the maintenance) of the identity of particular groups, whose intra- and inter-relations are typically regulated by the dynamics of the power relations manifested at the level of the individuals and the organization. The role of discipline is that of establishing a system of boundaries between the various groups that make up the whole, allowing to maintain a distance between the inside and the outside of the different groups (senior officers, junior officers, warrant officers, non-commissioned officers, etc.).

Lastly, a discussion of structuration of power in terms of resources can be traced back to Michael Mann's 1986 work on *Sources of Social Power*. The author identifies four sources, bases, or resources of power, defined as ideological, economic, military, and political. A more illustrative reinterpretation of this schemata is found in Clegg (1989), who argues for the so-called circuits of power, tasked with mobilizing relations of meaning and membership (ideological and political resources) and techniques of production and discipline (economic and military). Military power is a resource which breeds force, violence, and war (Machiavelli 1958; Giddens 1985). In relation to the previously discussed notions, force or power in the military is conceptualized in terms of techniques of discipline. While discipline is attributed a regulatory role in what concerns the internal dynamics of power and the recognition of hierarchy, in Clegg's view, military violence functions as a means to secure outcomes which cannot be achieved otherwise, e.g., through circuits of social integration, particularly against individuals or entities that are recognized as "others" or "outsiders" in terms of affiliation to the institution.

5 NATO and the ideology of power

This chapter examines the link between NATO ideology and discourse, with particular focus on the manner in which the Alliance's doctrine has been operationalized in the language of the most important NATO documents: the Washington Treaty and the (so far) eight strategic concepts. For the purpose of the present investigation of discourse as a form of communicative expression of the military organization, we shall look at ideologies as "systems of beliefs" or collective structures of ideas, notions, norms, and values, shared among the members of an organization.

5.1. Professional ideology and military values

When speaking about NATO ideology, one must agree to subordinate it to the broader terms of military or professional ideology. In this section, the discussion pivots on the conceptions that typify NATO as a military alliance stem from the set of values and shared representations that explicate the essential role the armed forces play as a powerful institution in any society.

Most members of modern military organizations are convinced that they are unlike the rest of the society. The very specific culture of the armed forces, their system of values, and their position of relative isolation within the society cause them to perceive themselves in a distinct way. Above all, the missions of the soldiers accentuate the impression of a difference from the rest of the national or international community. The fact that the military are eventually obliged to sacrifice their life for the fulfillment of higher objectives (military and political) contributes to the feeling of belonging to a class of their own, dissimilar to the civilian population. Although the military lifestyle has become closer to that of the rest of the population, especially over the past 50 years, this impression still persists within the institution. In a 2000 article published in the French military magazine, *Le Casoar*, Bernard Messana argues:

> Mais il est aussi juste de dire que se cultive dans l'armée, avec une sorte de délectation, un sentiment assez vif de différence voire même de supériorité morale. Choisissant le métier des armes un peu comme on entre en religion, par

vocation, acceptant en toute conscience le sacrifice suprême, investi du droit de donner la mort au nom des valeurs antiques – Patrie, Honneur, Courage, Devoir, Discipline – qui constituent son credo, le militaire se sent autre. (10)

It is also right to say that the army, with a kind of delight, cultivates a lively feeling of difference, even of moral superiority. By choosing the profession of arms as if one entered into religion, by vocation, deliberately accepting the supreme sacrifice, and invested with the right to offer their life in the name of ancient values – Motherland, Honour, Courage, Duty, Discipline – which constitute their credo, the military feel different. (Own translation from the original)

In the same vein, in her book *Values and Virtues in the Military*, Nadine Eggimann Zanetti argues that "military institutions are legitimized in terms of specific values and virtues: a purpose, which transcends individual self-interest in favor of a presumed higher good." (2020:30). Furthermore, the author considers that concepts such as "duty," "honor," "country," "courage," and "loyalty" illustrate the particular values and virtues that typify military institutions and set them apart from civilian ones, from the point of view of the organizational culture they adhere to (Eggimann Zanetti 2020).

The impression that the members of the military are different from the rest of society is cultivated in close association with the concept of identity of the social group that the armed forces constitute. Differentiation is indeed one of the elements that allows identification and, against this background, the particularly specific culture of the military, which largely supports the feeling of belonging and identity, emerges as extremely important. In particular, the system of values embedded in the military ideology has an important part in spreading the sense of belonging.

Military values can be defined as ideals and preferences that structure the representations and actions of the individuals of an organization and determine them to act in a specific manner. In this vein, military values become internalized beliefs and norms allowing the framing of both individual and collective behaviors and the creation of a strong connection between the people who share them. At the same time, this set of professional norms and values explain the relationship between the members of the military and constitute one of the factors determining the military's relations with other social groups and, more generally, with the rest of the national and international community.

The military organizations of the 21st century rely on the same model. The NATO, the most important security body of the present, functions as an integrated and coherent military body. This is mainly due to the fact that all composing armies share a military tradition, born between 1500 and 1900, at the time of the conquest of the world by Europe. After the end of the Middle Ages, all the Western armies experienced the same changes, albeit at different rates. According to the needs, objectives, and agendas of the governments, armed forces that were punctually raised at a specific moment gradually became permanent. Although initially private or semi-private, they were made public and placed under the orders of a sovereign power, thus acquiring the status of institutionalized community, and increasingly becoming more or less identified with the nation-state. Most of their characteristics come from this common heritage, which, to a certain extent, brings them close together.

In 1965, in a particularly comprehensive study of armies, Kurt Lang referred to what he considered to be the three most specific aspects underlying the military organizations. The first trait was the "community" character of military life. For the researcher, this community aspect means, above all, that the degree of control of the institution on all the aspects and phases of the privacy of its personnel is particularly important. He considered that such control was unrelated to what was practiced in civilian life. The second feature was the emphasis on "hierarchy." Evidently, all bureaucracies tend to use a similar power structure, but for Lang, this organizational form appears in its most accomplished aspect within the military institution. He considered that it could even provoke a certain authoritarianism in human-military relations. Finally, the last feature, closely related to the second, was the limited downward aspect of the chain of command. If information could trace the hierarchical structure from the base to the top, the orders and directives knew only one direction, the reverse. This structure of the chain of command has the unique function of ensuring the application of the orders. The fact that exchanges are rigorously regulated by a strict downward flow makes it possible to impose discipline and permanent control of the superiors over subordinates.

The discussed concept of military ethos and its functions generates the concluding statement that there is coherence and complementarity between the different military values. They seem logically articulated and tend to reinforce each other in order to better prepare the institution to face its goals, tasks, and missions. Against this backdrop, military ideology emerges as a set of values and beliefs amongst which duty, loyalty, respect, ultimate sacrifice, courage, honor, integrity, tenacity, solidarity, rigor, and respect for discipline and hierarchy appear particularly appreciated in military culture. In virtue of their profession, members of the military perceive this set of values as an exclusivity of their own organization, considering that no other socioprofessional category has developed similar ones.

5.2. NATO ideology and doctrine

The need for security has always been among the most continuously pursued goals of humanity. Historically, the world has experienced all kinds of wars and conflicts that put an end to entire civilizations while nurturing others. The world of the 20th century has also seen the two most devastating wars in human history. With Europe split and ravaged immediately after the end of World War II, it was only natural that order and security be reinstalled and safeguarded in the long run. When NATO was established in 1949, the post-World War II world was soaked in memories of the past but was also looking forward to a better and more promising future. There was a stringent need for a security organization that would both repair the damage of the past and build a long-lasting peace in the future. Against this background, NATO was founded as a security organization endowed with the appropriate political and military resources that would establish it as a guarantor of freedom and stability on the international scene.

Created in the aftermath of World War II as a response to the Soviet aggression, the NATO has served as the most coherent and structured organizational manifestation of a unified Western response to the security and ideological threat represented by the Soviet Union. Among the many roles NATO has assumed as a safeguard of international security, promoting and ensuring collective defense have been the most prominent ones. During the Cold War, from the founding of the Alliance in 1949 until the break-up of the Soviet Union in 1990–1991, the stated purpose of the transatlantic organization was to protect its members from external aggression, engage in diplomatic negotiation with its Eastern adversaries, and seek a peaceful resolution to East-West tensions. As the rationale behind of the establishment of NATO faded away until dissolution at the end of the Cold War, the Alliance was faced with the prospect of withering away, a scenario that imposed continuous reshaping of strategies and the promotion of new, more expansive conceptions of its form and function, way beyond its traditional purview. In the post-Cold war period, the Alliance continued to be a crucial actor in international politics and claimed for itself a dual role as a source and guardian of a new pan-European security system.

In order to achieve its stated goals, NATO had to remain faithful to an ideology that was flexible, but nonetheless relevant and enduring throughout its almost 70-year history. The previous analysis that linked knowledge and ideology has shown that the structure and the manifestation of ideology is culturally variable. Nonetheless, NATO has succeeded to bypass this inconsistency, fusing the ideological notions and the materializations thereof under the umbrella of a single organization, seen as a unified military body described as "collective defense organization, alliance of democracies, and security community" (Collins 2011:1). In a 2017 article published in *The Balance*, Kimberly Amadeo sees NATO as an international and, by excellence, a multicultural organization, which has constantly striven to reconcile multifarious ideologies under the overarching concept of collective security, succeeding in reaching a common ground for the construction, dissemination, and understanding of global safety issues, correlating various concepts of defense, most frequently challenged by historical, governmental, and strategic circumstances: freedom of the member countries, response to terrorism, regional stability, and transatlantic peace, most of which go beyond military might alone and need correspondence and alignment with the political and social ideologies of the present.

NATO is a continuously evolving organization whose identity is shaped by its members and through their interactions. Against the background of pluriculturalism, as an underlying aspect of a multinational organization such as the Alliance, I may further argue that military ideologies are relevant properties of military situations, regardless of the cultural context in which they are manifested.

The members of the military institution share the same ideologies and support different ideas that constitute the foundation of their own interpretation of the world, guide their understanding of events, and control their social performance. As they most frequently emerge from opposition and conflict, linguistically manifested by the polarization between "us" and "them," "ingroups" and "outgroups," and "positive" and "negative," ideologies monitor and control the attitude, behavior, and, in the long run, the actions of the organization in relation to the outside world. To wit, the pacifistic or belligerent ideologies of the military are manifested according to the geopolitical and geostrategic context and the mission statement of the armed intervention, and may be interpreted as positive or negative, based on the stance taken by the external observer.

Furthermore, as systems of ideas belonging to the same group, ideologies are the fundamental notions on which the social practices of the organization are based. This background also permits anchoring the concept of "doctrine," equally defined as a set of beliefs or tenets regulating perceptions about different matters. Consequently, military ideology is materialized in what is universally accepted as military doctrine, a formal expression of military knowledge, thought, and experience, defined as the actional dimension of a dogma.

Military ideologies are one of the most illustrative examples of constant systems of shared beliefs, which are enduring over time and independent of the political and social changes occurring in the world. Ever since the beginning of society, militarist ideology has been based upon the same steady pillars, reinforced by the same shared goals and objectives, that of supporting and defending the interests of the state and its citizens. Roughly put, although the term "military" has been broadly associated with the practice of war-making, modern history has pushed the term beyond its traditional limits into a more comprehensive contextualization of the meaning of combat, perceived as the joint efforts of multinational armed forces united by a common desire and ideal, and fighting as a single entity for a peaceful, conflict-free world.

On the other hand, and although conceptually based on firm ideological support, military doctrine is defined as a set of "concepts, principles, policies, tactics, techniques, practices, and procedures" that are only relevant at a given time, covering specific types of conflicts, their nature, the preparation, and the methods of engagement.[5] In the geopolitical and geostrategic context that has characterized the period between the foundation of the Alliance in 1949 and the present moment, NATO's doctrine has functioned as an authoritative guide, describing how the army thinks about fighting (the conceptual dimension) and guiding military activity (the actional dimension) by providing a common frame of reference across the Alliance. Moreover, the ideological guidelines encompassed in the doctrine link theory, history, experimentation, and practice, and aim at fostering initiative and creative thinking. The main purpose of having a well-stated doctrine at NATO level is to provide the Alliance with a firm body of statements on how the military forces should conduct a wide spectrum of operations and to establish a common lexicon which military planners and leaders can use in order to communicate effectively and efficiently.

5.3. Evolution of NATO's doctrine

A CDA of NATO discourse cannot be undertaken without approaching the issue under investigation from a wider perspective, the entry point being located at the intersection between ideology and language. To this aim, it is extremely relevant to examine the evolution of NATO's doctrine over the years so as to have a solid ideologically constructed context to be invoked when conducting the linguistic analysis.

NATO's doctrinary vision is officially expressed in a series of public documents, in the form of declarations and communiqués that account for the Alliance's decisions and reiterate the allies' support for aspects regarding NATO policies. These official documents are typically published in the aftermath of summit meetings, usually organized around significant moments in the Alliance's evolution and are, as Marian Dincă remarks in his 2012 book about the evolution of the North Atlantic Organzation, aimed at outlining proposals, introducing new policy, launching major initiatives, inviting new members, establishing new alliances, or reinforcing partnerships. The decisions are subsequently translated into action by relevant actors (the North Atlantic Council – NAC, the Nuclear Planning

---

5   Canada Department of National Defense. *The Conduct of Land Operations* B-GL-300-001/FP-000, 1998: iv–v.

Group – NPG, the Defense Planning Committee – DPC, the NATO-Ukraine Commission – NUC, NATO-Russia Council – NRC, and other subordinate committees or different command structures at NATO level) tasked with different responsibilities and operating in various areas of competency. NATO summits are always held in a NATO member country and are chaired by the NATO Secretary General.

A brief overview of the thirty-two NATO summits that have taken place since 1949 will shed light on the evolution of the Alliance's doctrine and will ultimately allow a better anchoring of the discourse analysis in the context outlined by the ideological landmarks that characterize the NATO, perceived as the international military institution of the 20th and 21st centuries. Within the framework of the present linguistic investigation, the texts of the documents made public after the high-level meetings are perceived as ideologically driven discourses which openly express the Alliance's stance in relation to key issues such as collective defense, massive retaliation, flexible response, force balance, East-West relations, cooperation, partnership, shared financial contributions, open-door policy, etc. The military documents as well as the public statements re-affirm the member countries long-standing commitment to actions aimed at a peaceful solution of disputes, at maintaining peace and security in the North Atlantic area, at expanding the Alliance through invitations of other members, and at pursuing an active policy in arms control, disarmament, and non-proliferation.

On the whole, our succinct analysis of the key concepts announced on the occasion of the summits leads to the conclusion that the doctrine orientations of the Alliance have remained constant over the years and have not suffered essential or radical modifications. Rather, NATO's doctrine has been periodically updated and adapted so as to respond to the nuanced challenges of the continuously and rapidly changing security environment.

5.4. Discursive representations of NATO's doctrine

NATO's doctrine could be defined as a collection of ideas, notions, principles, or plans that have been used to describe, rationalize, or justify the existence of the alliance. Due to the duality of the organization's stated purpose, these conceptions are also both political and strategic in nature. They are sometimes enunciated in detail, fixing institutional practices in discourse and ideological rhetoric, but most of the time, they are expressed in broad terms, ascribing to NATO's tasks and objectives not traditionally associated with alliances. They are often changed and adjusted to suit the specifications of the international configuration and therefore are extraordinarily diverse. Nevertheless, and despite their flexible nature, the conceptual pillars that fundament the Alliance's ideology have demonstrated their value and importance in keeping the allies bound and committed to a shared set of immutable values.

The role of rhetoric in the study of ideology is subsidized by the belief that language is a vehicle for human activity and plays an important role in rationalizing decisions and actions. Just like actions, words have consequences. Political and strategic language plays on and creates truth. Language is not merely a tool for the interpretation of events but, when used constantly, becomes part of a generally accepted political reality.

In conflicts, words are the main weapons and have often proved to be mightier than the sword. Wars inherently carry ideological features in that they are a clash between the good and the bad. Especially during the Cold War (when NATO's rhetoric was most galvanizing), senior allied leaders used language as determining factors in the perceptions, thoughts, and justifications of their actions. Sometimes dutiful and decorative, other times dull and ambiguous, the rhetorical expressions favored by NATO policy makers are directed toward the same goals: to inform, persuade, and express ideas about people, events, policy, objectives, and history. Discourse has always been the main medium for propagating conceptions about the nature and the promise of NATO. The language of the main NATO documents briefly summarized below helped inform an environment of threat and responses. The ideas expressed publicly by officials gave significance to the political and social events, to the policies pursued by the Alliance accordingly and served as a basis for both ideological beliefs and the practice associated with it.

5.4.1. The Washington Treaty

The end of World War II was a fertile ground for the gradual reactivation of the conflicts that had typified the relations between the Western powers and the Soviet Union ever since 1917. This "East-West" cleavage was further fueled by contradictory interests and conflicting political ideologies that materialized in disagreements over peace accords and compensations, while tensions reached boiling points during events such as the Berlin blockade in April 1948, the coup in Czechoslovakia in June 1948, or direct pressures on the independence of countries such as Norway, Greece, and Turkey. Against this background, Western European countries started to worry about the possibility of the Soviet Union spreading its power and ideology to several Eastern European countries. Since Western governments started to lessen their defense and discharged their military forces after the end of World War II, there was a growing need for a defensive regional alliance within the framework of the UN Charter, translated as a "treaty of alliance and mutual assistance," as British Foreign Secretary Ernest Bevin declared in January 1948. America started to sense the European anxiety from across the "pond" and adopted the Vandenberg Resolution in the Senate, thus allowing the United States to constitutionally participate in a joint defense system during peacetime. However, the United States agreed to offer military support only in case Europe were united. Seizing the opportunity, Belgium, France, Luxembourg, the Netherlands, and the United Kingdom signed the Brussels Treaty[6] in March 1948. This common defense accord aimed at strengthening ties between the signatories, an agreement which actually paved the way for what was to be later internationally recognized as the Washington Treaty.

Signed in Washington D.C., on April 4, 1949, the 14-article long agreement was ratified by 12 founding members (Belgium, Canada, Denmark, France, Iceland, Italy, Luxembourg, the Netherlands, Norway, Portugal, the United Kingdom, and the United States) and officially laid the foundations of the NATO. Deriving authority from Article 51 in the UN

---

6   The Brussels Treaty is a 10-article treaty of Economic, Social and Cultural Collaboration and Collective Self-Defense and was signed in Brussels, Belgium, on March 17, 1948.

Charter[7], the Treaty builds a sense of solidarity within the alliance and commits each member to share not only the benefits but equally the risks and responsibilities of collective defense – the fundamental concept of the Alliance, stipulated in the famous Article 5.

> The Parties agree that an armed attack against one or more of them in Europe or North America shall be considered an attack against them all and consequently they agree that, if such an armed attack occurs, each of them, in exercise of the right of individual or collective self-defense recognized by Article 51 of the Charter of the United Nations, will assist the Party or Parties so attacked by taking forthwith, individually and in concert with the other Parties, such action as it deems necessary, including the use of armed force, to restore and maintain the security of the North Atlantic area. Any such armed attack and all measures taken as a result thereof shall immediately be reported to the Security Council. Such measures shall be terminated when the Security Council has taken the measures necessary to restore and maintain international peace and security. (UN Charter, Article 51).

The main purpose for the establishment of the NATO was the need to provide a framework under which the Alliance could pursue its goals. The Washington Treaty is a brief but extremely instrumental document whose text encompasses the military ideology of the 20th century and forges it into discursive cohesion. The Treaty represents the verbalization of NATO's doctrine, shaped and supported by key values such as peace, democracy, stability, security, cooperation, dialogue, individual liberty, and the rule of law. The signatories of the Treaty openly express their determination to defend the liberties, cultural heritage, and the civilization of nations to endorse "stability and well-being" in the North-Atlantic region and to act in a unified manner in order to ensure "collective defense" and "the preservation of peace and security" (The North Atlantic Treaty, 1949).

However, the spare prose of the Treaty left enough space for maneuver for disagreements and distinctive interpretations among allies. Articles 3, 5, 9, and 13 are extremely relevant in this regard. Article 3, for instance, articulates the commitment to self-help and mutual aid. Its relevance resides in the power of the formulation to set the stage for a never-ending

---

7   Article 51 of the United Nations Charter acknowledges the right of independent states to individual or collective defense.

argument over one of the most contentious issues in the Alliance: the provisions of burden sharing, in terms of who should do what to make the Alliance a success. The article is by any means clarifying and has allowed polarizations between the Americans and the Europeans, who have constantly believed that the others should do more.

Second, the pledge in Article 5, that an attack on a member should be considered an attack on all, prompted the Europeans to assume that the United States would automatically come to the rescue in case of a Soviet attack. In turn, the Americans included a provision in Article 5 by which they made sure that their response is anything but automatic: "Each member will assist the Party or Parties so attacked by taking forthwith, individually and in concert with the other Parties, such actions as it deems necessary, including the use of armed force." In Chapter 12 of his 1977 book, *Time of Fear and Hope,* Escott Reid mentions that this qualifying phrase was introduced in Article 5 at American insistence, and that the United States would not have signed the Treaty had this qualification not been included. This clearly demonstrates the position of power from which the Americans negotiated the text and provisions of the Treaty.

Article 9 empowered the North Atlantic Council to create "such subsidiary bodies as may be necessary" for an operative application of the treaty. While the Americans saw this organizational apparatus as a means of prodding the Europeans to do more in terms of self-help, the Europeans considered it a way of entangling their U.S. partners in issues relating to European security. This concern remained valid for the following years and generated most of the conflicts that stamped the dynamics of power relations between the Americans and the Europeans.

With these controversial formulations in mind, it is important to note, however, that the remarks made at the signing ceremony by the representatives of the signatory member countries are significant in terms of rhetoric richness and for the general view that the men who signed the treaty truly believed in the universal values it encompassed. Flowery discourses promoted a positive and even idealistic vision of common security interests finally addressed by an official document.

Paul-Henri Spaak, the Belgian prime minister and minister for foreign affairs, described the treaty as "an act of faith in the destiny of Western civilization." Lester Pearson, the Canadian secretary of state for external affairs, declared that "our treaty is no mere Maginot Line against annihilation, no more foxhole from fear, but the point from which we start for yet one more attack on all those evil forces that would block our way to justice and to peace" (qtd. in Thomas 1997:23).

Gustav Rasmussen, minister for foreign affairs for Denmark, called it a "solemn reaffirmation" of the UN Charter, aimed at strengthening the system of the United Nations. Robert Schuman, the French minister of foreign affairs, called it "a sign of France's absolute determination to maintain peace." Italy, through the voice of its Foreign Minister Carlo Sforza, compared the treaty to the Magna Carta, a continuous creation that will be one of the "noblest and most generous events in human history" and characterized the text of the treaty as being "complex and articulate." The representative of Luxemburg, Joseph Bech, expressed optimism in the treaty's peace-making powers by hoping that "it may give the world a salutary period of lasting truce." Dirk Stikker, the Dutch foreign minister, shared Bech's vision and argued that the treaty marked "the birth of a new hope of enduring peace." The Norwegian foreign minister Halvard Lange also called it a "pact of peace," while, in the same vein, the Portuguese signatory representative José Cairo Da Matta characterized it as a "precious instrument of peace." On Britain's side, Ernest Bevin expressed a broader vision, in that the North Atlantic Treaty represented a step in the larger process of "enthroning and making paramount the use of reason against force." The American President Harry Truman closed the ceremonies by remarking that the treaty constituted "a solemn pledge ... a shield against aggression and the fear of aggression – a bulwark which will permit us to get on with real business of government and society" (24).

Besides being just propaganda surrounding the historical event, these comments reveal the commonly shared beliefs of the officials that Europe's internecine quarrels and hatreds would be finally extinguished and forever laid to rest by the positive collective force of the North Atlantic Community. In a prophetical revival of the ancient crusades, the Treaty and the rhetoric accompanying it reiterated the idea that only by banding together in common cause could Western civilization be saved from the communist hordes. In short, the document and the pomp of the ceremony can be regarded as a part of a larger effort to psychologically condition the North Atlantic nations for the ideological struggle that lay ahead.

The constancy and universality of the overarching vision expressed in the Treaty is demonstrated by the fact that, to date, the basic principles underlining the doctrine of the Alliance have not fundamentally changed nor has the Treaty been rewritten. The only "amendments" made so far are brought about by the series of accession protocols that have been appended as new members came aboard, and stem from the need to correlate current international concerns and objectives with national interests.

5.4.2. The Strategic Concepts

The military field can be considered to be eminently social and ideological at the same time. It functions according to specific social rules and is the legitimized medium for the manifestation of conflict, control, supremacy, and of different types of interests and power relations. In order to function properly, the military institution needs to be ideologically sensible and systematized. As an ideological group, the military institution disposes of clear formulations of ideologies, in the form of doctrines, or the so-called Strategic Concepts, explicitly defending the Alliance's ideology in a series of (public) documents openly made available to the community, be it political or civilian.

In the present social, political, and geostrategic setting, NATO, as *the* military organization of the 21st century, encapsulates a multinational force adhering to the same goal, stated and assumed as "collective defense," and defined as "an overall defensive concept for the North Atlantic Treaty area" (Collins 2011:42). Through its Strategic Concepts, NATO basically expresses "its view on the world and the threats it faced as a basis for developing its high-level strategy and to provide objectives and guidance to its military organizations to develop war plans" (41). While the military actions are a global set of procedures essentially conceptual in nature, we may further argue that the cognitive models used to represent the perception of the organization about the world are basically identifiable with ideology.

The Strategic Concepts are NATO's key documents, second only to NATO's founding North Atlantic Treaty in importance. They collectively reaffirm the Alliance's values and purpose and provide a comprehensive assessment of the security environment. These documents provide guidelines for the adaptation of the Alliance's military power to the ever-changing characteristics of the security environment, Since the end of the Cold War, they have been updated approximately every 10 years, to take account of changes to the global security environment. A series of eight Strategic Concepts have been issued to cover the three distinct periods that required a dynamic adaptation of the Alliance's strategic thinking: the Cold War period, the immediate post-Cold War period, and the security environment since 9/11, with more recent focus on the Russia-Ukraine escalating conflict.

From 1949 to 1991, a period spanning between the establishment of the Alliance and the end of the Cold War, the pivotal challenge was the bipolar confrontation between the East and the West, which resulted in the international relations being dominated by tension and hostility, to the detriment of cooperation and dialogue. Under these circumstances, a number of four Strategic Concepts were issued, encompassing the Alliance's vision in regard to the challenges of the security environment of that period and outlining its essential core tasks as a method of enacting NATO's fundamental ideology.

The first strategic guidelines were consolidated into "The Strategic Concept for the Defense of the North Atlantic Area, DC 6/1," approved by the NAC on January 6, 1950, a document whose general principles were subsequently supplemented by two more texts: MC 14/1 and DC 13.[8] The first overall strategic concept specified that NATO's main task was to deter aggression and that the engagement of NATO forces should only be activated in case deterrence failed and an attack was launched. Other key elements of this document included complementarity and standardization between the members of the Alliance. It was also stipulated that each member's contribution to defense should proportionally match its industrial, economic, geographical, and military capacity, and that resources should be ensured optimally. As compared to the USSR, the Alliance's

---

8   MC 14/1 was previously drafted as SG 13/16 "Strategic Guidance for North Atlantic Regional Planning" and formally endorsed by the Military Committee on March 28, 1950, under the current name. DC 13 was discussed by the Defense Committee on April 1, 1950 and passed under the title "The North Atlantic Treaty Organization Medium Term Plan".

military resources were numerically inferior. In order to compensate for this discrepancy, U.S. nuclear capabilities were invoked, in that the Alliance should "ensure the ability to carry out strategic bombing promptly by all means with all types of weapons, without exception" (DC 6/1, par. 7a).

The second Strategic Concept was developed after South Korea was invaded by North Korean divisions on June 25, 1950. This had an immediate impact on the Alliance's strategic vision which prompted the reexamination of the efficiency of NATO's military structures and the strength of its military forces. An integrated force was established under centralized command, and different structural changes were also implemented. These operational modifications, complemented by the accession of Turkey and Greece, had to be mirrored in a new Strategic Concept, which was drafted and approved by the NAC on December 3, 1952. The strategic documents needed updating and, consequently, MC 14 and DC 13 were merged in one single document, MC 14/1.[9] The text of the document was a comprehensive illustration of NATO's inclusive strategic approach, aimed at reinforcing defense of NATO areas.

The polarization between the allied forces and the Soviet Union is revisited in the discursive construction of one of NATO's objectives, which stipulates that one of the Alliance's strategic aims is "to destroy the will and capability of the Soviet Union and her satellites to wage war" (MC 14/1, par. 9). Overall, the second Strategic Concept followed the basic guidelines outlined in DC 6/1 and respected the same doctrine based on the core principle of collective defense.

It is only with the development of the third Strategic Concept that NATO's approach to defense took an essential turn. In the context of the United States and other European members' requests for a complete integration of nuclear policy into the Alliance's strategy, "MC 14/2 Overall Strategic Concept for the Defense of the NATO Area" is issued on May 23, 1957, introducing the doctrine of "massive retaliation," one of the key notions underlining the Alliance's new strategic orientations. MC 14/2 was accompanied by an explanatory document, "Measures to Implement

---

9   "Strategic Guidance" MC 14/1 was approved by NAC at the December 15–18, 1952, Ministerial Meeting in Paris.

the Strategic Concept," ratified under the title MC 48/2. Although advantageous from the perspective of reducing force requirements and, consequently, defense expenditure, this new concept was challenged by some of the Allies, who called for flexibility of using conventional weapons, which should be employed when dealing with minor forms of aggression, "without necessarily having to recourse to nuclear weapons" (MC 48/2, par. 6m(1)). Nonetheless, on the background of the still-existing tensions between the East and the West, NATO firmly opposed the concept of "limited war" in relations with the USSR: "...if the Soviets were involved in a hostile local action and sought to broaden the scope of such an incident or prolong it, the situation would call for the utilization of all weapons and forces at NATO's disposal, since in no case is there a concept of limited war with the Soviets" (par. 6m(1)).

The Soviets' political and economic activities also prompted NATO to readjust its strategy in case of out-of-area events, thus addressing concerns stemming from recent situations, such as the Suez crisis or the suppressing of the Hungarian uprising by the USSR in 1956. Consequently, in addition to the concept of "massive retaliation," the documents of the third Strategic Concept also reflected these apprehensions and the necessity to address them. "Although NATO defense planning is limited to the defense of the Treaty area, it is necessary to take account of the dangers which may arise for NATO because of developments outside that area" (Directive to the NATO Military Authorities from The North Atlantic Council CM (56)138, par. 7).[10]

In the context of the USSR's expanding atomic potential, NATO's competitive advantage in nuclear preemption weakened. European countries began to doubt the United States' will and potential to act as deterrent in case of a Soviet nuclear attack. Even more so, in 1961, the recent occupant of the White House, President J.F. Kennedy, openly expressed concerns regarding the provision of limited warfare and feared the possibility that

---

10 CM (56)138 is a political directive given from the NAC to NATO's military authorities on December 13, 1956. Issued six months before the ratification of the final form of MC 14/2, this document endorsed the implication of the Alliance outside its area of responsibility, thus creating a gateway for the inclusion of this provision in the (later) third Strategic Concept.

a nuclear exchange might be accidentally sparked. This was a turning moment in the strategic development of the Alliance, which was pressured into adopting a stronger non-nuclear posture and a more versatile strategy to supersede the increasingly questioned "massive retaliation" doctrine. As a logical consequence to these new tendencies, NATO initiated steps to adopt the fourth Strategic Concept, based on the newly introduced doctrine of "flexible response." On January 16, 1968, the Defense Planning Committee adopted the final version of the "Overall Strategic Concept for the Defense of the North Atlantic Treaty Organization Area," coded as MC 14/3. This new strategy incorporated two key features: flexibility and escalation. Paragraph 16c of the document specifies that the deterrent approach of the Alliance is based on a "flexibility that will prevent the potential aggressor from predicting with confidence NATO's specific response to aggression and which will lead him to conclude that an unacceptable degree of risk would be involved regardless of the nature of his attack" (MC 14/3, par. 16c). The strategy advocates three types of military responses in case of aggression: direct defense (if the enemy engaged in combat); deliberate escalation (a sequence of progressive steps to be taken parallel to the escalation of the crisis); general nuclear response (using nuclear power as the ultimate prevention). Just like in the case of the other strategic concepts, this one was also supplemented by a companion document, "MC 48/3 Measures to Implement the Strategic Concept for the Defense of the NATO Area," whose final form was issued on December 8, 1969. In the NATO Summit Guide, published in preparation for the Lisbon meeting in 2010, it is appreciated that the two texts that outlined the Alliance's fourth strategic concept were "so inherently flexible in substance and interpretation, that they remained valid until the end of the Cold War" (16).

The year 1991 marked the beginning of a new era. The Soviet Union, the United States' most dreaded enemy, was dissolved and the former adversaries, including Russia, became NATO members or partners. It was a thriving period for the Alliance, with peace and stability promoted through cooperation and dialogue. Since the end of the Cold War, NATO has presented four unclassified Strategic Concepts (Rome 1991; Washington 1999; Lisbon 2010; Madrid 2022), which enlarge the previously taken approach to safety and security. Unfortunately, and although the documents of the Strategic Concepts were declassified and made available to the public, the accompanying documents remain confidential.

NATO's first unclassified Strategic Concept was signed during the Summit organized in Rome, in November 1991. While it followed the same fundamental principle of "collective defense," outlined in the preceding texts, the 1991 Strategic Concept differed from the previous ones in that it was specifically aimed at enhancing and expanding European security through partnership and cooperation. The use of nuclear forces was reduced to a minimum, enough for the preservation of stability and security:

> This Strategic Concept reaffirms the defensive nature of the Alliance and the resolve of its members to safeguard their security, sovereignty and territorial integrity. The Alliance's security policy is based on dialogue; co-operation; and effective collective defense as mutually reinforcing instruments for preserving the peace. Making full use of the new opportunities available, the Alliance will maintain security at the lowest possible level of forces consistent with the requirements of defense. In this way, the Alliance is making an essential contribution to promoting a lasting peaceful order. (The Alliance's Strategic Concept 1991, par. 57)

The second unclassified Strategic Concept was adopted in April 1999, on the occasion of NATO's 50-year anniversary celebrated during the Washington Summit. Continuing the tradition of the members' commitment to common defense and security in the enlarged Euro-Atlantic area, this Strategic Concept was founded on a broader security approach which acknowledged the instrumental role of social, economic, and political aspects, as essential complements to the element of defense: "The Alliance is committed to a broad approach to security, which recognizes the importance of political, economic, social and environmental factors in addition to the indispensable defense dimension" (par. 25). Against the background of the newly identified multifaceted and multidirectional threats, including terrorism, human right abuses, ethnic conflicts, economic instability, political insecurity, and the delivery of nuclear, biological, and chemical weapons, the text of the document underlines the importance of cooperation and partnership as instruments for the preservation of security through consultation, deterrence, and defense. The strategy adopted on this occasion framed more flexible guidelines for NATO's forces, expanding the range of the Alliance's responsibilities so as to cover a wider spectrum of missions, comprising collective defense, peace support, and other crisis-response scenarios.

The two Strategic Concepts briefly described above are both supplemented by a classified military document MC 400 and, respectively, MC 400/2.[11]

In the aftermath of the terrorist attacks on September 11, 2001, the United States saw themselves exposed to the scourge of a newly emerged threat which brought to the forepart the need to defend NATO's populations both at home and abroad. Against this backdrop, in a report entitled "NATO 2020: Assured Security, Dynamic Engagement," former Secretary of State Madeleine Albright, the leader of the group of experts issuing recommendations, points out the necessity for the Alliance to be versatile and resourceful enough to operate far from home, thus suggesting a dramatic change in NATO's role to be envisaged in the new Strategic Concept. Adopted in Lisbon, on November 19–20, 2010, the current Strategic Concept illustrates the new orientations of the Alliance which has understood it was high time to revisit its mission, procedures, and plans and to be more adapted and anchored in the context of the realities of the modern security environment that typifies beginning of the new millennium (Dincă 2012). Under the title "Active Engagement, Modern Defense," the 2010 Strategic Concept reiterates the position of the Alliance as "a unique community of value committed to the principles of individual liberty, democracy, human rights and the rule of law" (par. 2) and reaffirms its commitment to counter today's threats: the proliferation of ballistic missiles and nuclear weapons, terrorism, cyber-attacks, and environmental problems. The core of the document consists in the presentation of the three essential tasks assumed by the Alliance in the following decade (defense, crisis management and cooperative security), in response to an increasingly fluid and globalized world:

> The modern security environment contains a broad and evolving set of challenges to the security of NATO's territory and populations. In order to assure their

---

11 MC 400 is known as "MC directive for the Military Implementation of the Alliance's Strategic Concept," issued on December 12, 1991. MC 400/2 was issued on February 12, 2003 under the name "MC Guidance for the Military Implementation of the Alliance Strategy".

security, the Alliance must and will continue fulfilling effectively three essential core tasks, all of which contribute to safeguarding Alliance members, and always in accordance with international law. (Active Engagement, Modern Defense – Strategic Concept for the Defense and Security of the Members of the NATO 2010, par. 4).

The document also describes NATO's commitment to promote international security by reinforcement of weapons control, disarmament, and by continuing its non-proliferation efforts and reiterates the Alliance's engagement to accelerate its reform and transformation process.

During its history of more than six decades during which it has undergone different stages of transformation, the North-Atlantic Alliance has changed its core strategy only five times: in 1952, 1968, 1991, 1999, and 2010. Starting with "The Strategic Concept for the Defense of the North Atlantic Area" in 1949, which was grounded on a large scale retaliation in case of a potential Soviet invasion, going through the guidelines of the concept of "massive retaliation," championed in 1952, an underlying principle which acted as a deterrent against possible attacks against any member of the Alliance, and then adopting the strategic concept of "flexible response," targeting hesitation and doubt in the mind of the prospective attacker as regards the strategic response, NATO's doctrine in the period before the Cold War culminates with the implementation of strategic measures aimed to ensure multidimensional security and promote cooperation, incorporated in the 1991 Strategic Concept. The Strategy elaborated in 1999 was the foundation of the military actions undertaken in Afghanistan and stipulated, among other principles, conflict prevention and crisis management, the development of Euro-Atlantic partnerships, policies of nuclear non-proliferation, and armament control.

Since the seventh Strategic Concept, issued at the Lisbon Summit 2010, the world has fundamentally changed. Russia's illegitimate annexation of Crimea in 2014 set in motion a series of events that culminated, in 2022, in a full-scale war between Russia and Ukraine. Peace in Europe was shattered, and the strategic competition was renewed. Since the beginning of the conflict in February 2022, Allies have expressed their determination to reset NATO's deterrence and defense for the longer term.

Keeping the three fundamental tasks (deterrence and defense, crisis prevention and management, and cooperative security) at its core, the 2022

Strategic Concept sets out a shared vision of the threats, challenges, and opportunities that require a constant adaptation of the Alliance to an increasingly dangerous and competitive world.

In a declaration that acknowledges the past, present, and future developments of NATO, an overarching statement connects the doctrinary vision that runs through all strategic documents ever issued by the Alliance: "Over time, the Alliance and the wider world have developed in ways that NATO's founders could not have envisaged, and these changes have been reflected in each and every strategic document that NATO has ever produced" (Strategic Concept 2022).

The Alliance's strategic thinking has undergone two distinct readaptations since 1949. They are marked by two historical periods: the Cold War era and the post-Cold War era. The 2022 Strategic Concept requires NATO to adjust to another phase of renewed geostrategic competition and provides a realistic assessment of NATO's deteriorated strategic environment. Like all the previous strategic documents issued before, the current Strategic Concept echoes the Alliance's traditional defensive scope and reiterates its long-lasting commitment to unity, cohesion, and solidarity, for a world where NATO is an indispensable actor that guarantees Euro-Atlantic security, peace, freedom, and prosperity.

5.5. Dimensions, aspects, and sources of power – toward an integrative framework

The study of power has long been the prerogative of political scientists and philosophers. Mere mention of the concept sends any scholar back in time, to the works of Niccolò Machiavelli (1958), Thomas Hobbes (2010), Max Weber (1947), Robert Dahl (1961), Michel Foucault (1980, 1982, 1983), Anthony Giddens (1985), Steven Lukes (2005), and a whole host of other scholars concerned with the philosophy of power. Topics discussed under the heading of power typically deal with the various forms of government, war and diplomacy, military structure and operations, etc. It is important for the context of the present investigation to note that power has traditionally been viewed as an attribute of large social entities and/or of the relations between them.

This section aims at locating different concepts of power against the background of NATO's military ideology, while focusing on the interaction between its members, whose dynamics are very conclusive in terms of identifying the key moments that have contributed to the cohesion or to the division of the North Atlantic Organization. "Alliances are as old as the states themselves," Wallace Thies remarks in his 2009 book, *Why NATO Endures,* "but the way their members act toward each other has changed greatly over the past several centuries" (120). The central element that stimulates interaction between the members of any alliance is the ongoing struggle for power. The dynamics of power relations are a productive source of transformation of alliance members from rivals to partners sharing common values and interests. Historically, the fluctuations in the balance of power within NATO have stemmed from "changes in the scope and pace of warfare, changes in the distribution of power among the leading states, and the presence of absence of divisive ideological issues" (121).

The bipolar power structure that developed in the aftermath of World War II and the ideological divide that polarized the Western world and the Soviet Union deprived military and political leaders of flexibility in terms of choosing alliance partners. For Western European states, only the United States could assume the role of shield against the invasion of communist ideologies and against the security threat represented by the Soviets. By acknowledging the double superpower structure that opposed the United States and the Soviet Union, most of the former great powers in Europe (Great Britain, France, Germany) also accepted the idea that they were no longer in a position to compete for supremacy with either of the two major leading states. Moreover, given the ideological split between the East and the West, the states in Western Europe became increasingly aware of their common goals and interests. Since they no longer viewed each other as rivals in a struggle for preeminence, the members of the North Atlantic Alliance came together out of the belief that it was better "to encourage rather than frustrate each other's plans to regain military supremacy, to increase rather than restrict the power of their allies and to push each other forward rather than hold each other back" (124).

From the very beginning, the configuration of the Alliance comprised a collection of states that were differently positioned internationally: one superpower, several middle powers, and several small powers. At the time the Atlantic Alliance was formed, the objective of the American officials was to hold the United States aloof from entangling commitments while offering the minimum necessary in pledges of support. The idea behind the Americans' limited involvement was to stimulate the Europeans to restore the European balance of power, while the United States was left free to pursue its own global interests. Nonetheless, the development of a collective defense has proven irregular over the years and was so often far from the initial expectations set by the powers involved in it. British officials were hoping for an alliance modeled on World War II partnership between the United States and Great Britain, with the two countries providing leadership to the continental members. However, during its evolution, the Alliance has grown into a structure in which the British were reduced to the status of secondary power and became one of the many contributors to the American-led organizational machinery. The French were anticipating using the alliance in order to gain access to American money and equipment as a means of rebuilding their own forces and continuing to support their colonial empire. Much of their dreams were shattered and, for most of the time, the French behaved as the most important antagonistic power in the Alliance, challenging not only the supremacy of the United States but also the very notion of a European defense based on American support, which they have struggled to eliminate and replace with de Gaulle's vision of a "European Europe." The Germans were the most compliant with the American-led strategies, often lend their support unconditionally and used the framework of the Alliance to push for and finally obtain reunification, and, consequently, a strong status as continental power within NATO.

The power dynamics of the relations between the most important states in the Alliance (The United States, Great Britain, Germany, and France) will be further investigated against a framework of power definitions, conceptually supported by the identification of various dimensions, aspects, and sources of power. Furthermore, the power relations theories that inform this section of the book can definitely constitute the basic framework for a further, more complex and targeted analysis of the ideological changes experienced by the NATO throughout its almost 70-year history and the manner in which they impacted on the power dynamics between NATO member states.

Thinking about power in unitary terms to which all theorizations must be subjected is too limited an approach to be taken by anyone who investigates the notion of power from the perspective of its multilayered structure. Against such a view, this section will argue for several distinct and yet related dimensions of power, analyzed in terms of their internal relations and also in terms of the interdependence existing between them, with back-and-forth references to the different conceptualizations of power throughout history. All the mentioned theories will be used to identify manifestations of power specific to NATO and will be used to establish the context for the linguistic analysis of military discourse.

Kenneth Boulding (1989) divides power into three major categories, drawing on the nature of consequences it entails: threat power, exchange power, love power. Destructive power, associated with the behavior of threat, manifests in specific contexts in which one (or more) of the agents (henceforth referred to as A) control the use of destructive power against persons or structures that weaker actors (henceforth named B) value. There are many sources for threat, ranging from the most objective, such as starvation or potential death, where responsibility is voluntarily expressed, to the most personalized and subjective sources which question the individual's basic mechanisms for coping with the social realities.

The dynamics of threat depend, to a great extent, on the response given to it. The degree of threat individuals might experience is related to the degree of power that can be exercised over them. Boulding further argues that whether it is implicit or explicit, threat "always involves some sort of communication" (1989:25). The most common response to threat is submission. As long as B fulfills A's demands, threat is not followed through. In the absence of this threat-submission dichotomy, it would be very difficult to organize social life and, inherently, social relations. A descriptive large-scale example in this direction is the attitude of defeated nations in wars: imperial powers have always exercised different forms of power over the colonies they conquered. In society, it is illustrative for the dynamics of power relations between parents and children, teachers and students, employers and employees.

A second destructive reaction to threat is counterthreat. In this scenario, the threatened party has, or convincingly pretends, to hold its own means of destruction. The dynamics of this relation throws the ball back in the court of the threatener, who has a choice of two possible responses: either carry out the threat or not do so. Nonetheless, both types of reaction entail a sequence of subtle and often unpredictable consequences. Counterthreat leads into a situation of deterrence, which is a highly unstable but prevalent characteristic of international structures and the current reason for increased military expenditure. An organized system of deterrence is based on the cooperation of nations of relatively equal technology and threat power. The role of the military within such a system is either to prevent war from breaking out or win a war once it has broken out. Here, the concept of relative power is more important than absolute power. In the dynamics of military power, relativity translates into the latent dimension of power. In the context of NATO's deterrence policies, latent power is defined as power that does not exist at a specific moment, but that has the potential for being activated later on. The concept of power as deterrence has been extensively exploited by NATO's strategic documents, especially in official papers where there was an obvious need to define, delineate, and specify the understanding of the notion and its practical application in different scenarios.

Among the general objectives of the defense concepts outlined in NATO's 1949 Strategic Concept is the need "to coordinate, in time of peace, our military and economic strength with a view to creating a powerful deterrent to any nation or group of nations threatening the peace, independence and stability of the North Atlantic family of nations" (5). Glenn Snyder (1959) identifies two major types of deterrence which are wrapped around the concepts of power as threat and power as denial. In a nutshell, deterrence by threat of punishment relies on the U.S. threat of nuclear retaliation against the Soviet Union, while deterrence by denial relies on conventional and tactical nuclear forces capable of defeating Soviet aggression on the battlefield. In February 2010, a Department of Defense *Ballistic Missile Defense Review Report* stressed the importance of deterrence for the United States strategy, in that "deterrence is a powerful tool, and the United States is seeking to strengthen deterrence against these new challenges" (6). A few months later, this vision was encapsulated by the 2010 Strategic Concept: "We will ensure that NATO has the full range of capabilities necessary to deter and defend against any threat to the safety and security of our populations" (15). In 2014, in a Pentagon briefing on missile defense, Admiral Winnefeld reinforced Snyder's earlier conceptualizations of deterrence, by reevaluating the two identified types: "… the fact of the matter is that deterrence exists in two forms. One is denying an adversary's objectives. The other is imposing costs if they – if deterrence fails" (par. 31).

Another operationalization of the concept of deterrence distinguishes between central and extended deterrence. The definition proposed by Justin Anderson and Jeffrey Larsen describes central deterrence as "preventing aggression or coercion against one's vital interests, including the homeland, by threatening to punish and/or defeat an adversary or to thwart his aggression," while extended deterrence refers to "providing protection to an ally or security partner via comparable deterrent threats – threats of punishment and/or threats of denial, also known as threats of operational defeat" (2013:xi). What anchors the concept of deterrence in our discussion about power is its strategic value, which presupposes assuming a decision to use all state power, including military force. I see it as a means by which NATO asserts its power outside the organization, in case of crisis.

In the light of the recent Ukraine conflict which has brought critical changes to the European security environment, with Russia undertaking aggressive actions against its neighbors and threatening the United States and its NATO Allies, the concept of deterrence has once again been brought into the limelight. The words "deter" or "deterrence" each appeared only once in the Washington Summit Communiqué, the main strategic document of 1999, but the term seems to have made a remarkable comeback, populating the discourse of the 2016 Warsaw Summit Communiqué 37 times, under different morphological variations: "deter," "deterrence," "deterrent." This is a clear indication that NATO policies needed a revamping, in a context in which the Alliance has to secure its power to counteract possible threats coming from the lifelong enemy in the East.

Given the background of belligerent practices, such as those associated with military action, we agree with Boulding in that threat power may be seen as productive, in the sense that it has the capacity of producing means of destructions (weapons, guns), but it can also have an integrative dimension, especially when the threat is carried out by a group or an organization (an army), which must adhere to a moral code in order to function.

It may be argued that this destructive dimension of power that encompasses threat is subject to pathology, mainly stemming from the notion that certain organizational structures must have an enemy that rationalizes their existence. The armed forces of a nation are the most situated example in this context since they emerge as national defense organizations.

To a larger extent, NATO is the international defense organization, basically defined as a collection of such national institutions, structured against potential enemies. In order to authorize and validate their existence, military organizations need an enemy; if they do not exist, the defense organization tends to invent them "as being necessary to their own legitimacy and justification" (Boulding 1989:69).

A rather extremist view of power as threat could be traced back to Machiavelli's definition of the concept, which he primarily associates with violence. In S.S. Wolin's 1960 book entitled *Politics and Vision*, the chapter on Machiavelli and his "economy of violence," explains the essence of Machiavelli's concept of power: "... the hard core of power is violence and to exercise power is often to bring violence to bear on someone else's person or possessions" (220). In *The Prince*, the Italian 16th-century scholar offers a profuse descriptive account of power viewed in terms of strategy. Four centuries later, Clegg links back to the same idea, concluding that "strategies must practice an economy of violence, which requires careful consideration of its military forms, knowledge of the means required to translate armed bodies into disciplined organized power" (1989:33).

The term "violence" is used to illustrate a dimension of power that employs force. Thomas Schelling postulates that there is a conceptual variance between violence and force in that force is the use of physical compulsion in a way that directly carries out the end to be desired, while violence is the use of pain for punishment, coercion, and negotiation (1970). Neither of the two terms is explicitly employed in military documents; however, referring to the armed power as "military forces," "Alliance forces," "conventional forces," "appropriate force structures," "defense forces," "bulk of forces," "multinational forces," "reaction forces," and "nuclear forces" is a clear indication that the etymological source for the image of the military nowadays stems from the notions of force and violence as they had been conceptualized 500 years ago.[12] Procedures might have changed, with diplomacy and negotiations superseding brute force, but the activating mechanisms are still based on power.

Another dimension of power, with the notion of knowledge at its core, encapsulates a wide array of different and yet related types of power, initially identified by John R.P. French, Jr., and Bertram Raven (1959). In addition to the reward and coercive types, situated in Samuel Bacharach and Edward Lawler's (1981) taxonomy under sanctional power (branching out as coercive, remunerative, and normative power), French and Raven mention legitimate, referent, and expert power. These three types of power could be grouped under one dimension, that of knowledge. Considering knowledge and information as sources of power is extremely important for the present analysis of power dynamics in military discourse. Any method of communication and all communicative strategies and patterns characteristic to an organization are imbued with discursive manifestations of norms, values, codes, and standards – a collection of knowledge-based elements deeply anchored in the cultural and social practices of that community. In trying to build a cogent theoretical framework, the eclectic combination of concepts that has been analyzed, albeit overlapping, function as a solid foundation for well-established sources of power. Furthermore, this imbrication of notions offers even more insight into the recognition of knowledge as a base for power. Against this background, concepts such as legitimate power, expert power, and referent power come to shape the knowledge dimension of power.

Legitimate power stems from acceptance and internalization of core values, a dynamic process in which A influences and dictates B's attitude and behavior. Sociologists such as Max Weber (1947) or Herbert Grice and Edward Shils (1939) attach legitimate power to the concept of authority, which is ascribed to a dominant ideology and recognized as such. In discussing the nexus of ideology, discourse, and power, I have already referred to Van Dijk's definition according to which ideology is as group-shared knowledge. Consequently, I can argue that, in virtue of the intricate

---

12 The examples are taken from The Allianc's Strategic Concept, April 1999.

relation between knowledge and power, ideology becomes instrumental in exercising power and authority within a group or organization.

In the military, the notion of legitimacy of authority definitely involves generally shared knowledge, in the form of some sort of code, or standard, accepted by the individual, by virtue of which the stronger agents can assert their power, especially with the help of formal rules and by means of a hierarchical flow of authority. Legitimacy is a cognitive or perceptual phenomenon. Weber sees it as a "belief in the appropriateness of the authority structure" (1947:45). Judgments about that appropriateness are made in relation to moral values, normative ideals, and pragmatic or utilitarian criteria. The bases for legitimate power are cultural values, acceptance of social structure, and the existence of a legitimizing agent.

At the level of NATO as a military organization, the most prevalent values are embedded in the cultural hegemony of the member states, which share the power of prescribing behavior among themselves, aiming toward a unified structure and centralized manifestations of power. The fact that NATO headquarters – the political and administrative center of the Alliance and permanent home of the North Atlantic Council's decision-making body – has been located in different cultural and historical hubs since 1949 (London, between 1949 and 1952, Paris, between 1952 and 1967, and then Brussels, since 1967) may actually be indicative for the acknowledgment of the respective countries' strong values and historically acknowledged position within the organization.

Another basis for legitimate power is the acknowledgment of social structure. As long as the social construction of a group, organization, and society is accepted, legitimate authority will be validated. Even more so, when the structure involves a hierarchy of authority, legitimate power in an organization, the size of NATO becomes mainly a relationship between offices and departments rather than individuals. It might be debated that, in this case, legitimate power also involves the perceived right of a particular person to hold the office. Remark accepted, we will defend our holistic approach by arguing that the present analysis focuses on the organization as a system, not on the discrete or rather individual elements composing it, which would represent a totally different approach that does not constitute the purpose of this work.

Designating and recognizing a legitimizing agent also endorses legitimate power. Like in any other structured organization, political and strategic decisions in NATO are taken on the basis of a delegating system, made up of decision-making representatives from the member countries, who meet regularly and take consensual decisions. Therefore, legitimization of agency is a well-rooted, acknowledged, and endorsed practice not only across all levels of the organization but also outside of it. In the words of Lord Ismay, NATO's first secretary general, the main role of the Alliance after its establishment was to act "as a forum for consultation" with the precise purpose of countering anti-NATO and communist propaganda, "based on a firm and universally accepted concept of the purpose and techniques of preparing the civilian front" (1954:153–155). NATO was conceived as a force of positive change, the agent legitimizing the founding members' commitment for collective defense, an organization whose ideology was imbued with moral force directed toward forging new patterns of thought in Europe and beyond it.

What links Weber's previously mentioned theory regarding the appropriateness of authority with the notion of knowledge as a dimension of power is that, in addition to accepting the authority of a superior, subordinates must also accept the rationale for it. Such justification stems from the expert dimension of power. Evaluating and accepting expertise is primarily a cognitive process that entails social influence. Expert power is a fundamental source of power dynamics and has the potential to change behavior. It involves both effective communication strategies and content-based information, which is judged to be valid and accepted as such, either based on credibility or on the logic of arguments. However, the extent of expert power is somehow restricted, since it is limited to cognitive systems and because the expert is perceived as being endowed with superior knowledge or abilities in very specific areas, making his power constrained exclusively to these areas. The dynamics of expert power are based on a flow of specialized information that circulates both inside and outside the organization.

NATO is undoubtedly a source of expert power, the holder of specialized information that underpins a whole array of associated practices, embraced, and endorsed by civilian and military societies altogether. Internally, expert power is recognized as a prerogative of the legitimized agents – and this is where clear-cut delineations between legitimate and expert power disappear – who are tasked with establishing rules, norms, guidelines, policies, and doctrines. Outside the organization, expertise is a resource employed to control information and the degree of exposure of the civilian society to it. Examples in this direction are located in analyses investigating different types of propaganda or the relation between media and the military.[13]

It is well known that the United States has always been viewed as the expert power within the Alliance, especially when drafting NATO's early strategies. For example, the Alliance's nuclear strategy relied heavily on the American atomic monopoly to deter Soviet aggression. The U.S.-led initiatives in this regard emphasized the application of the "trip-wire" concept (justifying the presence of U.S. troops in Europe as a trigger for Strategic Air Command bombers in case of a Soviet attack) or of the "shield concept" (explaining the sharing of atomic secrets with Britain and accounting for the placement of nuclear weapons in Europe under U.S. custody). In the spring of 1963, the American officials were the ones promoting the establishment of the multilateral force (MLF) as an ultimate fix to alleviate European military anxieties.[14] Later on, in 1967, the 1950s Dulles-sponsored concept of "massive retaliation" was substituted with the strategy of "flexible response" also at the initiative of the Americans.

Morton Deutsch and Harold Gerard (1955) semantically equalize expert power to informational power. Their synonymy leads to the argument

---

13 As early as 1953, NATO had established an information program which would offer tours of NATO and Supreme Headquarters to journalists, students, and politicians. Propaganda also included films, such as *The Atlantic Community: Know Your Allies* or *Alliance for Peace* and the publishing of the *Information Letter* (later *NATO Review*) and *The NATO Handbook*. In the increasingly technologized 21st century, NATO has aligned with the modern world in using social media as an instrument for promoting transparency. A simple search on Google by the keyword "NATO" would direct visitors to the organization's site, a virtual agora for the dissemination of a significant volume of (old and new) information about the Alliance.

14 The MLF was a sea-based force consisting of 25 jointly owned, financed, and controlled allied surface ships, each armed with Polaris missiles and manned by mixed crews.

that this additional dimension refers to influential power that stems from content and form alike. Suffice it to say, at this stage, that the adaptation of military language to the framework of contemporary communication has constituted a constant concern within the organization. In *On Escalation: Metaphors and Scenarios,* Herman Kahn observes that most of the terminology used to discuss national security issues has often been judged as "conceptually inadequate, inconsistently used, or even emotionally biased" (1965:275). Since terminology difficulties affect professionals and the public alike, the challenge in terms of communication has been to improve this situation by clarifying concepts and notions, by making clear distinctions of terms, by increasing the number of shared understandings and explicit formulations. The following chapter will be partly dedicated to this semantic analysis, where lexical polarizations and explicit versus implicit meaning will be perused in detail.

Another type of power, subordinated to the concept of knowledge, and whose dynamics is worth investigating, is referent power. This dimension of power is positioned at the intersection between concepts such as status, identity, membership, and affiliation. It basically discusses the desire of social agents to identify with the most powerful referent, an association which is galvanized by a stronger cognitive and behavioral image of the dominant power, which becomes a model to look up to and to wish identification with, in virtue of its superior knowledge (expertise and legitimacy). Leon Festinger argues that the affiliation is driven by the weaker power's need to conform to the same "social reality" of the dominant group, a practice which results in the adoption of the stronger power's cognitive structure, in terms of adhering to the same set of norms, perceptions, values, beliefs, and, ultimately, ideology (1950:279). It basically results in the weaker power adhering to the same universe of knowledge, by embracing the same social representations and cognitive models that are the foundations of ideological discourse. Moreover, the weaker actors constantly seek to maintain the status quo of this relationship by believing, behaving, and talking like the dominant power, an emulation by which social and cognitive models are being morphed into discursive practices. The stronger the identification, the greater the referent power and the more powerful the discourse.

From this perspective, NATO is to be perceived as a reference group exerting relational power. It is the very definition of the term "alliance," in all political, strategic, and even lexical meanings, which directs to the notion of organization, defined as an organized structure, composed of member states relating and interacting in virtue of their affiliation, or, on a more subjective note, of their desire to be identified and acknowledged as a coalition, a collection of powers, i.e., individual states that aspire to have a seat at the roundtable where decisions are made for the mutual benefit of all parties involved.[15] The foundation of the North Atlantic Organization rests on the notion of treaty perceived as a motive force, a hub of reference with binding power. In 1948, Canadian statesman Louis St. Laurent observed that the idea of the proposed North Atlantic Treaty "would create the dynamic counter attraction to Communism," with the aim of propelling Europe toward "a free, prosperous and progressive society, as opposed to the totalitarian and reactionary society of the Communist world" (House of Commons Debates 1948/4:3449). Against this background, it is obvious that the newly found organization was aiming to function as a referent power in the hope to attract the "weaker" actors, i.e., the oppressed and disaffected states of the Communist bloc, into a closer, more stable, and more secure association. The opposition formulated here is inherently ideological.

Perhaps one of the key concepts underlining the dimension of referent power is the notion of relation. To some extent, it might find itself embedded in the definition ascribed to reference power, at least in that affiliation and membership inherently presuppose some kind of relationing. Albeit this blurred theoretical delineation, we will define the relational dimension of power as a separate concept, first and foremost because it appears to be constructed based on the imbrication of multiple layers, of which notions such as "unity," "community," "dependence,"

---

15 Since the foundation of NATO, in 1949, there have been 29 NATO summits, with the last one taking place in 2017 in Brussels. NATO summit meetings provide periodic opportunities for Heads of State and Government of member countries to consult, evaluate and provide strategic direction for Alliance activities, to introduce new policy, invite new members into the Alliance, launch major initiatives and reinforce partnerships.

"interdependence," "partnership," or "exchange" emerge as the most noteworthy.[16]

One of the fundamental political axioms of the Cold War was that a united community of North Atlantic nations would be a strong organization tasked with promoting and preserving peace. In an address to the Congress on June 12, 1950, Dean Acheson, the United States Secretary of Defense in the Truman administration and one of the key players in the creation of the North Atlantic Organization, remarked: "In our unity, there is strength. And in our strength, there is unity" (931). His axiomatic reasoning is a clear indication of the Alliance's first envisaged objectives, focusing on creating an entity organized around the basic principle of power.

The importance of the relational dimension of power as a pillar for the interactions that typify the dynamics of a group resides in the acknowledgment of the organic character of a community, defined as an evolving entity composed of individuals who lead a common existence under some organized form of shared social and political principles. A community acquires the dimension of identity only based on the dynamics of the inherent relations that manifest inside it. What made the North Atlantic Community a successful concept was the fact that did not emerge through force (as opposed to the Soviet-dominated community) but based on shared values, cultural legacy, and consensus. In 1951, referring to the importance and nature of the relations established within NATO, Acheson observes that "The North Atlantic Treaty is far more than a defensive arrangement. It is an affirmation of the moral and spiritual values which we hold in common" (527). The power of the relations that were built among nations in the Alliance has proven to be more far-reaching in its implications, testifying to the value and significance of community-based actions and shared intentions. Besides acting as a unified entity toward collective defense, the

---

16 Aspects regarding the rhetoric of relational power in NATO's evolution from community to partnership have been discussed during the International Conference *Literature, Discourse and Multicultural Dialogue*, Section: Language and Discourse, and published in the Proceedings of the Conference. (Arhipelag XXI Publishing House, Târgu Mureș, 2017 (Iulian Boldea, Editor), pp. 431–439, eISBN 978-606-8624-12-9).

North Atlantic Community has been engaged in pursuing an active role in the attainment of political and social objectives of NATO. One among many examples of acknowledgment of this phenomenon can be traced back in the Final Communiqué of the North Atlantic Council Meeting in February 1952, in Lisbon:

> The partnership between the nations of the North Atlantic Treaty is not just for defense alone but for enduring progress. The members of the Council look forward to the time when the main energies of their association can be less concentrated on defense and more fully devoted to cooperation in other fields, for the well-being of their peoples and for the advancement of human progress. (par. 1)

The symbiotic bond between NATO and the concept of an Atlantic Community was in time transformed into a synonymous relationship. NATO's raison d'être was to defend the Atlantic Community, a term that conjured up a group of nations with shared values, interests, and objectives and whose power exponentially grows as it is fueled by the strength of the relations that are being created and nurtured within the organization.

Against this backdrop, social exchange and dependence are two interrelated concepts at the intersection of which we can find, once again, the notion of power. Dependence and interdependence constitute the departing point in analyzing power, in that exchange cannot occur without these two relations, and parties could not operate and obtain an outcome in isolation. J.W. Thibault and H.H. Kelley (1959) observe that dependence exists when an actor's outcome is contingent not only on his own behavior but also on what others do simultaneously or/and in response to the actor's behavior. What makes the dependence dimension of power relevant in this context is its inconsistent dynamics. The mechanism of dependence varies across relationships and settings and is considered to be one of the most resourceful aspects of power dynamics in organizations.

At the beginning of the 1960s, R.M. Emerson (1962) and Peter Blau (1964) formulated a power-dependence theory by postulating that, in addition to being a foundation for social relationships in general, dependence is also the footing of each of the other actor's power in a relationship. The implication of this principle is that power constitutes an intrinsic aspect of relationing, and becomes a function of dependence, in that the power of an actor stems from the other actors' dependence. Taking this rationale further in the context of our discussion of NATO and power dynamics, it might be argued that the Alliance is an actor which acquires, promotes, and enforces power in virtue of the network of dependence relationships it creates and fosters.

Similar to any other relational structure, NATO has founded its early conceptions on the sense of dependence, grounding it on principles such as outcome alternatives and outcome values. The main impetus that drove the very notion of alliance, back in the days when the Washington Treaty was signed, in 1949, and even before that, during the Washington Talks, the previous year, was the belief that better outcomes are more likely to be obtained by joining a network than in isolation. By the same token, outcome value is what leads different actors to attach values or priorities to the various effects of a given relationship. The greater the value attached to the outcome, the greater the power. And since outcome alternatives and outcome values are considered essential for the collective security of the modern world, NATO has imposed itself as one of the greatest and most powerful organizations of the present and the highest institutional embodiment of the Western humanist concepts of unity.

Although it clearly emerged as a reaction to the Soviet threat in the context of postwar dynamics (Soviet Union was the "villain" who was at that time perceived as having the ideological power that needed counteraction), the rationale behind the creation of a North Atlantic Community was elucidated by the need to preserve unity and promote the higher ideals of Western civilization. In the mid-1950s, there was a shift in conception which placed more emphasis on "cooperation *for* something rather than merely against something" (Dulles 1956:708). John Foster Dulles's use of the indefinite pronoun may refer to a quite ambiguous task, but in the context in which he gave the address at the annual luncheon for the Associated Press in April 1953, the notion prompted directly to a change in conception which was basically a smooth transition from dependence to interdependence. In his speech, the U.S. Secretary of State referred to NATO's earlier potential to act as a counteraction to communism being complemented by the newly envisaged task of reflecting the spirit of Western civilization. This serves as an example of one of the earliest manifestations of NATO's relational power, put at use in an effort to heal disunity in Western Europe. The goal of promoting relations of interdependence between the nations of Western Europe was justified by the need for organizations such as NATO to act as permanent guardians of long-range peace and not only provide emergency ties in times of crisis. The search for permanency in transatlantic relations tilted the balance toward the intra-Western political purposes which were no longer tied to the Soviet threat. This new focus would urge the transformation of a military alliance into a stronger political reality. To this purpose, as stipulated in the 1956 *Report of the Committee of Three on Nonmilitary Cooperation in NATO*, member countries were encouraged "to make consultation in NATO an integral part of the making of national policy" (par. 44). With the example of the Suez crisis in mind, allied leaders were prompted to combat the acrimonious forces that might manifest in organizations such as the Alliance.[17] In truth, as Thomas points out, "the intent of this rhetoric was to restrain the members of NATO from embarking on future military adventures without consulting the other allies, and especially the United States" (1997:59).

Political implications aside, this new orientation in NATO's strategy stands witness to the importance of relational power and the dynamics of dependence and interdependence. Ties within the alliance became stronger and the concept of interdependence implied that the member countries shared the responsibilities of interaction. This vision made the need for joint action become imperative, stemming from the axiomatic rationale that the security of North America and Western Europe were inseparably linked. Ideologically, the notion carried further meaning and helped give more contour to the U.S.-Soviet polarization. It embedded a contrastive

---

17 The Suez Crisis took place in late 1956, when Egypt was invaded by Israel, followed by the United Kingdom and France, which aimed at regaining Western control of the Suez Canal and ousting Egyptian President Gamal Abdel Nasser from power. However, due to the political pressures of the United States, the Soviet Union, and the United Nations, the three invaders were forced to withdraw. The episode humiliated Great Britain and France and strengthened Nasser's power in the region. One of the implications of the Suez Crisis was the tarnished image of Great Britian, which had to admit its decline as a super power. In the aftermath of the crisis, it became clear that the two world superpowers (the United States and the Soviet Union) were more than ready to get fully involved in any conflict and affirm their power in any issue that had an immediate impact on their interests.

appreciation of the two antagonistic powers: while the Soviets and their allies had attained strength and unity through dependence and domination, NATO pursued the same objective through interdependence.

Nonetheless, one downside of the interdependence theory can be observed in situations where the shared power may acquire subjective relevance for the actors involved. This aspect becomes critical because it implies the cognitive factor of power relationships. Since actors often lack complete information on the dimension of interdependence or available resources, the use of power is based not only on the objective conditions of the relationship but also, and more importantly, on the judgment actors make about these conditions. The manifestation of interdependence is the criteria by which different actors interpret and synthesize the wide array of conditions underlying power relations. This argument is relevant in the context of the decision-sharing principle that underlies all NATO decisions, offering participants a proper context for their subjective, interest-driven assessment of different issues at stake, in virtue of the dynamics of their status and access to resources within the organization. One particularly illustrative example of a situation where actors used their subjective evaluation of position and made independent judgments about the power in use could be found in the dynamics of the discussions during the Ministerial Meeting of the North Atlantic Council in Athens of May 1962, when the United States and the United Kingdom, as the most powerful nuclear members of the Alliance, called in the non-nuclear Allies for consultations regarding the role of nuclear weapons and the procedures relating to their usage.[18]

---

18 On May 5, 1962, the foreign and defense ministers organized a joint meeting in Athens to discuss concepts related to Cold War deterrence in the context of the ongoing polarization between NATO and the Soviet Union. The participants in the meeting represented the United States, the United Kingdom, France, Belgium, and Greece. The purpose of the meeting was to give the non-nuclear Allies a consultative role in decisions over the use of nuclear weapons. The two main issues the participants had to agree upon were the role of the Alliance in the nuclear deterrent and the maintaining of a balance between nuclear and non-nuclear forces. Although the main guidelines of the meeting received consensual evaluations and response from the contributors, there were some issues that were treated as a bone of contention by the partakers. United Kingdom expressed

In this particular case, negotiating interpretations of the policies associated with the use of nuclear weapons was an exercise of power dynamics with a positive outcome. Reaching a common ground during the Athens talks created a relational framework which provided a basis for the actors' perception of their own power, of the likelihood of other actors'' making use of theirs and for the common evaluation and selection of multiple tactical and strategic options. This example is indicative of the assumption that power-interdependence theory is grounded on dual-role parameters, which are simultaneously a source of integration and of conflict. The negotiation of the dimension of interdependence ultimately determines whether parties wish to be part or stay in a given relationship if they can change it by discourse or action or if they consciously accept to position themselves to a certain distance in the relationship.

The concept of power as exchange is also a dimension of power embedded in the relational approach. Drawing on Boulding's theory, we may assert that insofar as it defines formal or contractual agreement and reciprocity, the relations established at the level of the Alliance are based on exchange. In the simple form of trade, Boulding informs, "A gives B something and B gives A something" (1989:27). But exchange goes beyond the mere definition that relates it to trade, and the wider conceptualization of exchange involves other mechanisms such as discursive negotiations, conversation and debates, reciprocal services, etc.

In social sciences, power is associated with the dynamics of social exchange. Social power, Van Dijk argues, "is a property of the relationships between groups, classes or other social formations, or between persons as social members" (1989:19). David Baldwin develops the concept of power as social exchange and argues that "all exchange relationships can

---

doubts regarding the need to increase the Alliance's non-nuclear capabilities; France considered immoral to ask the Allies to build up non-nuclear troops, while the adversary (the Soviets) would still have the tactical advantage and advocated powerful means of deterrence; Belgium felt the need to address these issues in detail, probably because the concept might have needed clarifications from their perspective and they felt the need to have a more informed opinion before offering an answer; Greece, on the other hand, was not interested in defining guidelines for nuclear weapons usage.

be described in terms of conventional power concepts" (1978:1229). Central to Baldwin's argumentation of power is the dimension of authority he aligns with Blau's (1964) viewpoint, which explains authority from the prism of the relations between individuals and the collectivity, or between different members of an institution, in virtue of their ideological affiliation and organizational membership.

In what concerns the power interactions at the level of the North Atlantic Organization, the notion of exchange is an integrative positive-sum relationship, in which all parties benefit while having the feeling of belonging to a structured mechanism that not only asks but also gives back. One application of the earlier discussed notion of interdependence as a dimension of power dynamics can be located in the concept of burden share. The concept translated into task sharing in defense, greater specialization of the functions of different members of the Alliance, and a division of labor to overcome the rising costs and complexities of the armament. In his first message to the North Atlantic Council, on February 15, 1961, President J.F. Kennedy referred to the importance of burden sharing, stressing the need for the allies to "establish principles...on which burden-sharing can be based" (333). This is an indication of the political endorsement of the concept of interdependence, whose applicability invoked the extension of the American global leadership in partnership with the European allies. From this point on, interdependence became the conceptual and practical linkage between economic, political, and military policies. Even more so, this relation suggested that the United States would attempt to use trade and arms agreements as bargaining chips to win allied support for the burden sharing in Europe and Asia. In its crudest form, the promotion of this link allowed Washington to exert its sanctional power while fashioning a framework of incentives and penalties aimed at convincing the allies to embrace its vision and actions. It was discursively motivated by the belief that an economic, political, and military partnership between Western Europe and the United States "will further shift the world balance of power to the side of freedom" (71).

However, the concept of burden share will prove as unifying as divisive for NATO member countries. Ever since the initial talks about new security arrangements in Western Europe, in the form of the British initiative back in 1947, it was taken as a given by the signatory parties that there would be a pooling of resources by the democratic states, following the example of the cooperation between the United States and Great Britain during World War II. The issue of who would contribute how much proved the most contentious. The Europeans believed that the Americans should do most of the work, while they were free to concentrate on economic recovery. The United Stated promoted the idea that their European allies should give more, since the Americans were already burdened to a degree that could not be sustained indefinitely. In his 2009 book *Why NATO Endures,* Wallace Thies argues that the burden shifting grew more enticing especially when the allies agreed to set up an integration coalition force, which entailed a balance in the burden sharing: the larger the forces contributed by the United States, ~~the lesser of those~~ the fewer those required from the Europeans, and vice versa. With the United States being the most powerful member of the Alliance, it was only natural that the Americans would want to reduce the burden upon their forces while seeking to transfer the ability to do more and ultimately bear most of the burden of taking care of themselves, once economic recovery had been achieved, to the Europeans. By and large, burden share has been one of the essential points of consultation between NATO member states, with most of the annual reviews of the Alliance's force goals focused on burden shifting, in virtue of the belief that the more one member could be persuaded to contribute, the less that would be required of the rest of the allies.

The tripartite integration of economic, political, and military power was the pillar of the transition from interdependence to partnership, anchoring the relational power of the Alliance even deeper within an increasingly dynamic framework. When applied at the intersection between economic, political, and military interests, the concept of interdependence not only designates this tendency but also helps promote its growth. The idea of partnership envisioned a partial decline in the relative responsibility and implicitly influence of the United States, translated as a cognizant encouragement by a major world power of the growth and expansion of a co-equal power. However, this proposed shift in the power balance did not have the desired effect, and despite the fact that in August 1962, Britain and West Germany had declared their initial support, the concept was criticized by the reluctant French and European and American observers alike as being a mask for U.S. hegemony (Hoffman 1963).

Kennedy's promotion of an Atlantic Partnership was not new, and it was interpreted as being a revival of the pluralist vision of the postwar world envisaged by George Kennan's dumbbell concept in the late 1940s.[19] It was a clear indication that the United States was willing to share power among the members of an alliance assembled around the core notion of equal rights and responsibilities. Such a vision implicitly acknowledges the importance of strong connections between greater and smaller powers united in a common cause – collective security. The essence of the relational power embedded in the very notion of a Transatlantic Alliance is expressed and explained throughout its journey from community to interdependence and finally to the solid partnership it represents today.

---

19 George Kennan's dumbbell concept promoted the view that an economic and political alliance is stronger if it has been agreed to by partners of equal weight on both sides.

Conclusion

This monograph's main aim was to offer a framework of analysis tailored specifically for a critical investigation of the ideology of power as it is linguistically illustrated in the military discourse of the NATO. The entire approach draws on the traditional postulation that ideologies are created, maintained, and practiced through language. By merging a critical view on discourse with the analysis of ideological values, the suggested investigative methodology focused on the tridimensional relation between language, ideologies, and the notion of power.

CDA, the proposed method of analysis, has proven to be an extremely fertile ground that encouraged the development of new approaches of language analysis, aimed at raising awareness about the prevalent social and political issues of today. By recommending CDA as an efficient approach, we also support the notion that this method has a well-defined role in social sciences. For the purpose of this research specifically, using CDA has greatly facilitated the construction and deconstruction of discourses, by guiding an informed exploration of communication in collective social institutions, such as NATO, and by providing a generous framework of analysis of the discursive means by which the reality is critically interpreted and understood.

Military discourse – the object of investigation — has been conceptualized from a broader perspective that defines it as an essential tool for shaping and transmitting the identity of the military organization of the present. Starting from a general discussion of military communication and narrowing down the analysis to NATO military discourse, reified in official texts and documents that the Organization has produced since 1949 has proven instrumental in locating a wide array of ideological landmarks that typify this form of linguistic expression. Predominant concepts such as security, defense, cooperation, crisis management, etc. are glued together by the overarching notion of power, which is salient in the Alliance's discourse, throughout its almost 75-year evolution.

A generous portion of the present study was dedicated to uniting ideology, discourse, and power through a coherent analysis of the functions of ideologies and of the role they play in structuring discourses. The notion that ideologies function as vectors of power is illustrated and maintained by a thorough analysis of NATO's doctrine, through an approach that connects military values to professional ideologies with the goal of identifying and discussing different dimensions, aspects, and sources of power underlying military communication in NATO.

Pertinent conclusions can be drawn from the analysis of different types and sources of power in an organization and in NATO as a particular example. Of the various types of power presented in the book, three types emerge as being specific to the Alliance: relational power, adversarial power, and predominant power.

For NATO, relational power can be defined as one's ability to influence specific bilateral or multilateral relationships. The dynamics of relational power as manifested in NATO discourse can be seen as a concert of forces which serve several purposes:

✓ They shape and control the security environment both within NATO and outside it;
✓ They generate a unified vision of common values and security objectives;
✓ They maintain and nurture internal and external cohesion.

In the context of the current analysis, adversarial power would translate as opposing attitudes and viewpoints and the legitimacy of such manifestations inside the Alliance (between members states which have often displayed antagonistic stances before reaching consensus) and, more explicitly, between NATO and external entities, in such contexts where the Alliance has opposed the courses of action taken by different states or actors (the USSR, Russia, terrorist organizations).

The discussion about predominant power can start from an axiomatic principle: the greater the basis for power, the greater the power. This theory could explain the source of the United States' status as a superpower worldwide and leading power in the Alliance. Especially in regard to NATO and the United States, legitimate, expert, and referent power are the broadest in range. They function not only to endorse the influence of the North Atlantic Organization in relation to other security institutions but also to fundament the authority exercised by the United States within the Alliance. Finally, the more legitimate the source of power, the less resistance it produces. This hypothesis accounts for the Americans' being at the leadership of the Alliance since its early history, prescribing doctrine and fixing strategies and concepts both in discourse and in practice, while the other NATO powers followed their lead. However, throughout the history of the Alliance, the leadership of the United States has often been challenged, and it is this opposition that has generated the dynamic and fluctuant pattern of relations between NATO member countries.

This monograph was dedicated to articulating a theory of ideology in relation to the notion of discourse, approached from cognitive, social, and linguistic perspectives. It also sought to offer a clear conceptualization of the notion of power, and to adapt the general theories about power to the specificities of NATO as a military organization. NATO's discourse becomes the legitimate locus for the identification of different frameworks of power, whose dynamic manifestations have a direct impact on the ideological and discursive evolution of the Alliance and on the power relations it fosters within and outside its borders.

Language is not power, but it definitely encodes power. The present work may be considered a springboard for future investigations of the ideology of power as it is reified in military discourse. Further exploring the language that typifies NATO discourse – materialized in the Alliance's official documents, issued on different occasions, by planning groups, committees, and councils – will definitely yield a rich crop of power relations. Decision-making in organizations has a lot to do with framing ideology. In this context, the dialectical relationship between words and actions could be investigated from the perspective of power and its essential role in galvanizing military and political will. Further research could be dedicated to discovering a pattern in power dynamics at NATO level, based on the multilayered framework proposed in this book. The main types of power discussed in this work (integrative, adversarial, and predominant) could be investigated from the perspective of their linguistic materialization, through both qualitative and quantitative methods of analysis. The idea that power can be located at the intersection between language and ideology is not new. Nonetheless, NATO's discourse is worth exploring at least with the aim of discovering whether it represents an essential mechanism for the construction of the ideology of power.

Works Cited

Acheson, Dean. "The North Atlantic Pact: Collective Defense and the Preservation of Peace, Security and Freedom in the North Atlantic Community." *Department of State Bulletin*, 27 Mar. 1949.

———. "Address to Congress." *Department of State Bulletin*, 12 Jun. 1950.

———. "Address to Congress." *Department of State Bulletin*, 1 Oct. 1951.

———. "Address to Congress." *Department of State Bulletin*, 5 Jan. 1953.

Adler, Katya. *Ukraine War: Russia Atrocities bring NATO Members Closer.* 26 November 2022. https://www.bbc.com/news/world-europe-63754799. Accessed 28 Nov. 2022.

Anderson, Justin V. et al. *Extended Deterrence and Allied Assurance: Key Concepts and Current Challenges for U.S. Policy.* USAF Institute for National Security Studies, 2013.

Arendt, Hannah. *On Violence*. The Penguin Press, 1970.

Baldwin, David A. "Power and Social Exchange." *The American Political Science Review*, Vol. 72, 1978, pp. 1229–1242.

Bellenger, Lionel. *Le talent de communiquer*. Nathan Publishing House, 1989.

Blommaert, Jan. *Discourse (Key Topics in Sociolinguistics)*. Cambridge University Press, 2005.

Bloor, Meriel, and Thomas Bloor. *The Practice of Critical Discourse Analysis. An Introduction*. Hodder Arnold, 2007.

Boulding, Kenneth. *Three Faces of Power*. Sage Publications, 1989.

Cameron, Deborah. *Working with Spoken Discourse*. Sage Publications, 2001.

Chertoff, Michael. "The Ideology of Terrorism: Radicalism Revisited." *The Brown Journal of World Affairs*, Vol. XV, no. 1, 2008, pp. 11–20.

Chouliaraki, Lili, and Norman Fairclough. *Discourse in Late Modernity: Rethinking Critical Discourse Analysis*. Edinburgh University Press, 1999.

Clegg, Stewart R. *Frameworks of Power*. Sage Publications, 1997.

Collins, Brian J. *NATO. A Guide to the Issues*. Praeger, 2011.

Cook, Guy. *Discourse*. Oxford University Press, 1989.

Daldal, Asli. "Power and Ideology in Michel Foucault and Antonio Gramsci: A Comparative Analysis." *Review of History and Political Science*, Vol. 2, no. 2, 2014, pp. 149–167.

Dulles, John F. "Address at the Annual Luncheon for the Associated Press, 1953." *Department of State Bulletin*, 30 Apr. 1956.

Eggimann Zanetti, Nadine. *Values and Virtues in the Military*. Berlin, Germany: Peter Lang Verlag, 2020.

Eyal, Jonathan. "NATO's Enlargement: Anatomy of a Decision". *International Affairs (Royal Institute of International Affairs 1944–)*, Vol. 73, no. 4, Oct. 1997, pp. 695–719.

Fairclough, Norman. *Analyzing Discourse: Analysis for Social Research*. Routledge, 2003.

———. "Critical and Descriptive Goals in Discourse Analysis." *Journal of Pragmatics,* Vol. 9, no. 6, 1985, pp. 739–763.

———. *Critical Discourse Analysis*. Addison Wesley, 1995.

———. *Discourse and Social Change*. Polity Press, 1992.

———. *Language and Power*. Pearson Education, 2001.

Fairclough, Norman, and Ruth Wodak. "Critical Discourse Analysis." *Discourse as Social Interaction*, edited by Teun A. Van Dijk, Vol. 2, Sage Publications, 1997, pp. 258–284.

Festinger, Leon. "Informal Social Communication." *Psycological Review,* Vol. 57, 1950, pp. 271–282.

Foucault, Michel. *Power and Knowledge. Selected Interviews and Other Writings 1972–1977*. Pantheon Books, 1980.

———. "Subject and Power." *Critical Inquiry,* Vol. 8, no. 4, 1982, pp. 777–795.

Freshwater, Ed. "COVID 19: Why We Need to Ditch the Military Terms." *Nursing Standard*, 2020, https://rcni.com/nursing-standard/opinion/comment/covid-19-   why-we-need-to-ditch-military-terms-160071. Accessed 20 May 2021.

Gamble, Teri K., and Michael Gamble. *Communication Works*. McGraw-Hill, 2013.

Gramsci, Antonio. *Prison Notebooks,* Vol. 1. Translated by Joseph A. Buttigieg. Columbia University Press, 1992.

Habermas, Jurgen. *Erkenntnis und Interesse.* Suhrkamp, 1977.

Hidalgo Tenorio, Encarnacion. "Critical Discourse Analysis, an Overview." *Nordic Journal of English Studies,* Vol. 10, no. 1, 2011, pp. 183–209, http://ojs.ub.gu.se/ojs/index.php/njes/article/view/658/609. Accessed 21 Aug. 2016.

Kahn, Herman. *On Escalation: Metaphors and Scenarios.* Praeger, 1965.

Kennan, George. "A Fateful Error." *New York Times,* 5 Feb. 1997, p. A23.

Kennedy, John F. "President Pledges U.S. Support of NATO." *Department of State Bulletin,* 6 Mar. 1961.

Krings, Hermann et al. *Handbuch Philosophischer Grundbegriffe.* Kosel, 1973.

Kristeva, Julia. *Desire in Language: A Semiotic Approach to Literature and Art.* Columbia University Press, 1980.

Linell, Per. "Discourse Across Boundaries: On Recontextualizations and the Blending of Voices in Professional Discourse. *Text,* Vol. 18, no. 2, 1998, pp. 143–157.

Lord Ismay, Hastings L. *NATO, the First Five Years 1949–1954.* NATO archives online.

Machiavelli, Niccolò. *The Prince.* Everyman, 1958.

Marcus, Solomon. *Comunicarea internaţională ca sursă de conflicte.* Political Publishing House, 1985.

Messana, Bernard. "Rapport Armée-Nation dans la perspective de la professionnalisation. Réflexions d'un observateur candide." *Le Casoar,* no. 159, octobre 2000, p. 10.

Oddo, John. *Intertextuality and the 24-hour News Cycle: A Day in the Rhetorical Life of Colin Powell's U.N. Address.* Michigan State University Press, 2014.

Oneţ, Alina-Elena, and Ana-Blanca Ciocoi-Pop. "Covid War(s)? The Influence of Military Rhetoric on Government Discursive Practices during the Coronavirus Pandemic." *The Land Forces Academy Review,* Vol. 27, no. 1, 2022, pp. 39–44.

Parsons, Talcott. "On the Concept of Political Power." *Proceedings of the American Philosophical Society,* Vol. 107, no. 3, 1963, pp. 232–262.

Porter, James E. "Intertextuality and the Discourse Community." *Rhetoric Review,* Vol. 5, no. 1, 1986, pp. 34–47.

Potter, Jonathan. "Discourse Analysis and Discursive Psychology." *Qualitative Research in Psychology: Expanding Perspectives in Methodology and Design*, edited by Paul M. Camic et al., American Psychological Association, 2003, pp. 73–94.

Ralph, Stuart, and Mark Stoove. "Using Military Language and Presence Might Not Be the Best Approach to COVID and Public Health". *The Conversation*, 2021, https://theconversation.com/using-military-langu age-and-presence-might-not-be-the-best-approach-to-covid-and-public-health-166019. Accessed 11 Nov. 2022.

Rogers, Rebecca, editor. *An Introduction to Critical Discourse Analysis in Education*. Lawrence Erlbaum Associates Publishers, 2004.

Rotaru, Nicolae. *Comunicarea în organizațiile militare.* Tritonic Publishing House, 2005.

Sadan, Elisheva. *Theory and Practice of People-Focused Social Solutions.* Hakibbutz Hamenchad Publishers, 1997.

Stoddart, Mark C.J. "Ideology, Hegemony, Discourse: A Critical Review of Theories of Knowledge and Power." *Social Thought and Research*, Vol. 28, 2007, pp. 191–225. doi:10.17161/STR.1808.5226.

Taylor, Stephanie. "Locating and Conducting Discourse Analytic Research." *Discourse as a Data: A Guide for Analysis,* edited by Margaret Wetherell et al., Sage Publications, 2001, pp. 5–48.

Thomas, Ian. *The Promise of Alliance: NATO and the Political Imagination*. Rowan and Littlefield Publishers, Inc, 1997.

Van Dijk, Teun A, "Critical Discourse Studies. A Sociocognitive Approach." *Methods of Critical Discourse Analysis,* edited by Ruth Wodak and Michael Meyer, Sage, 2009, pp. 62–86.

———. "Ideology and Discourse Analysis." *Journal of Political Ideologies*, Vol. 11, no. 2, 2006, pp. 115–140.

———. "Politics, Ideology, and Discourse." *The Encyclopedia of Language and Linguistics*, Vol. 9. Pergamon Press, 2004, pp. 728–740.

———. "Critical Discourse Analysis." *The Handbook of Discourse Analysis,* edited by Deborah Schiffrin et al., Blackwell Publishing, Blackwell Reference Online, 2003a, pp. 352–371.

———. "The Discourse-knowledge Interface". *Critical Discourse Analysis. Theory and Interdisciplinarity*, edited by Gilbert Weiss and Ruth Wodak, Palgrave Macmillan, 2003b, pp. 85–110.

———. "Discourse Analysis as Ideology Analysis." *Language and Peace*, edited by Chistian Schäffner and Anita Wenden, Darmouth Publishing, 1995a, pp. 17–33.

———. "Discourse Semantics and Ideology." *Discourse and Society*, Vol. 6, no. 2, 1995b, pp. 243–289.

———. "Ideological Discourse Analysis." *New Courant*, Vol. 4, no. 1, 1995c, pp. 135–161.

———. "Structures of Discourse and Structures of Power." *Annals of the International Communication Association*, Vol. 12, no. 1, 1989, pp. 18–59. doi.org/10.1080/ 23808985.1989.11678711.

Van Dijk, Teun A. and Walter Kintsch. *Strategies of Discourse Comprehension*. Academic Press, 1983.

Vygotsky, Lev S. *Thought and Language*. Newly revised. Translated and edited by Alex Kozulin, M.I.T Press, 1986.

Weiss, Gilbert, and Ruth Wodak, editors. *Critical Discourse Analysis*. Palgrave Macmillan, 2007.

Widdowson, Henry G. *Text, Context, Pretext. Critical Issues in Discourse Analysis*. Blackwell, 2004.

Winnefeld, James. Transcript: Admiral James A. Winnefeld at 2014 Missile Defense Conference, https://www.atlanticcouncil.org/comment ary/transcript/admiral-winnefeld-at-2014-missile-defense-conference/. Accessed 1 Nov. 2022.

Wodak, Ruth. "Does Sociolinguistics Need Social Theory? New Perspectives on Critical Discourse Analysis." Keynote Address *SS2000*, Bristol, 27 April 2000, www.univie.ac.at/linguistics/forschung/wittg enstein/unemploy/handoutbristol11.htm. Accessed 13 Oct. 2021.

Wodak, Ruth, and Christoph Ludwig. *Challnges in a Changing World*. Passagen Verlag, 1999.

Wodak, Ruth, and Michael Meyer. "Critical Discourse Analysis. History, Agenda and Methodology." *Methods of Critical Discourse Analysis*, 2nd ed., edited by Ruth Wodak and Michael Meyer, Sage Publications, 2009, pp. 1–33.

Wolin, Sheldon S. *Politics and Vision*. Little, Brown, 1960.

NATO official documents

CM (56)138 – Directive to the NATO Military Authorities from The North Atlantic Council, 13 December 1956.Report of the Committee of Three on Nonmilitary Cooperation in NATO, 13 December 1956, www.nato.int/archives/committee_ of_three/CT.pdf. Accessed 10 Nov. 2017.

DC 6/1 – The Strategic Concept for the Defence of the North Atlantic Area, 1 December 1949.

DC 13 – A Report by the Military Committee on North Atlantic Treaty Organization Medium Term Plan, 1 April 1950.

Final Communiqué of the North Atlantic Council, Lisbon, 20–25 February 1952.

Madrid Summit Declaration, 22 July 2022, https://www.nato.int/cps/en/natohq/official_texts_196951.htm?selectedLocale=en. Accessed 15 Nov. 2022.

MC 3/5 – The Strategic Concept for the Defence of the North Atlantic Area, 3 December 1952.

MC 14/1 – A Report by the Standing Group on Strategic Guidance, 9 December 1952.

MC 14/2 – The Overall Strategic Concept for the Defense of the North Atlantic Treaty Area Organization, 23 May 1957.

MC 14/3 – The Overall Strategic Concept for the Defense of the North Atlantic Treaty Area Organization, 16 January 1968.

MC 48/2 – A Report by the Military Committee on Measures to Implement the Strategic Concept, 23 May 1957.

MC 48/3 – Measures to Implement the Strategic Concept for the Defence of the NATO Area, 8 December 1969.

NATO 2020: Assured Security; Dynamic Engagement. 21 May 2018, https://www.nato.int/strategic-concept/strategic-concept-report.html. Accessed 21 Oct. 2021.

NATO 2002 Strategic Concept, 29 June 2022. https://www.nato.int/cps/en/natohq/topics_56626.htm. Accessed 15 Nov. 2022.

NATO's response to Russia's Invasion of Ukraine, 18 October 2022. https://www.nato.int/cps/en/natohq/topics_192648.htm. Accessed 12 Nov. 2022.

NATO's Response to the COVID-19 Pandemic, February 2021, https://
www.nato.int/nato_static_fl2014/assets/pdf/2021/2/pdf/2102-factsh
eet-COVID-19_en.pdf. Accessed 18 Oct. 2022.

North Atlantic Treaty, Washington, 4 April 1949.

Non-NATO official documents

Ballistic Missile Defense Review Report, 1 February 2010, https://archive.
defense.gov/bmdr/docs/BMDR%20as%20of%2026JAN10%200630_
for%20web.pdf. Accessed 11 Sep. 2018.

UN Charter, San Francisco, 1945, https://treaties.un.org/doc/publication/
ctc/uncharter.pdf. Accessed 14 May 2018.

Bibliography

Abercombie, Nicholas et al. *The Dominant Ideology Thesis*. Allen and Unwin, 1980.

Afrim, Constantin, and Mircea Cosma. *Comunicarea eficientă în conducerea operațiilor Forțelor Terestre*. "Lucian Blaga" University Publishing House, 2015.

Agabrian, Mircea. "Comunicare și percepție în organizația militară." *Spirit militar modern 4–6*, 1994, pp. 8–11.

Amadeo, Kimberly. *What Is NATO?,* 26 September 2022, https://www.thebalancemoney.com/nato-purpose-history-members-and-alliances-3306116. Accessed 15 Oct. 2022.

Bacharach, Samuel B., and Edward J. Lawler. *Power and Politics in Organizations*. Jossey-Bass Publishers, 1981.

Bakhtin, Mikhail. *The Dialogical Imagination*. University of Texas Press, 1981.

Blau, Peter. *Exchange and Power in Social Life*. Wiley, 1964.

Blommaert, Jan, and Jef Verschueren. *Debating Diversity: Analyzing the Discourse of Tolerance*. Psychology Press, 1998.

Boucek, Cristopher. "Counter-Terrorism from Within." *RUSI Journal,* Vol. 153, no. 6, 2008, pp. 60–65.

Bouzon, Arlette. *Comunicarea în situații de criză*. Tritonic Publishing House, 2006.

Britton, Bruce K., and Arthur C. Graesser. *Models of Understanding Text*. Psychology Press, 2014.

Calleo, David. *Beyond American Hegemony: The Future of the Western Alliance*. Basic Books, 1987.

Cameron, Deborah. *Working with Spoken Discourse*. Sage Publications, 2001.

Chomsky, Noam. "A Minimalist Program for Linguistic Theory." *The View from Building 20*, edited by Kenneth Hale and Samuel J. Keyser, MIT Press, 1993, pp. 1–52.

Clark, Hebert H. *Using Language*. Cambridge University Press, 1996.

D'Andrade, Roy. *The Development of Cognitive Anthropology*. Cambridge University Press, 1995.

Dahl, Robert A. *Who Governs? Democracy and Power in an American City*. Yale University Press, 1961.

Derrida, Jacques. "Structure, Sign and Play in the Discourse of the Human Sciences". In *Writing and Difference*, Routledge, 1967, pp. 278–294.

Deutsch, Morton, and Harold Gerard. "A Study of Normative and Informational Influences Upon Individual Judgement." *Journal of Abnormal and Social Psychology*, Vol. 51, no. 3, 1955, pp. 629–636.

Dincă, Marian. *Evoluția Alianței Nord-Atlantice văzută geopolitic și geostrategic*. University of Oradea Publishing House, 2012.

Duranti, Alessandro, and Charles Goodwin. *Rethinking Context: Language as an Interactive Phenomenon*. Cambridge University Press, 1992.

Eagleton, Terry. *Ideology. An introduction*. Verso, 1991.

Emerson, Richard M. "Power-dependence Relations." *American Sociological Review*, Vol. 27, no. 1, 1962, pp. 313–327.

Farr, Robert, and Serge Moscovici. *Social Representations*. Cambridge University Press, 1984.

Fauconnier, Gilles. *Mental Spaces: Aspects of Meaning Construction in Natural Language*. MIT Press, 1985.

Fauconnier, Gilles, and Mark Turner. *The Way We Think: Conceptual Blending and the Mind's Hidden Complexities*. Basic Books, 2003.

Fiske, Susan. T, and Shelley E Taylor. *Social Cognition*. McGraw-Hill, 1991.

Foucault, Michel. *El discurso del poder*. Folios Ediciones, 1983.

French, John R., Jr., and Bertram H. Raven. "The Bases of Social Power." *Studies in Social Power*, edited by David Cartwright, University of Michigan Press, 1959, pp. 232–256.

Gadamer, Hans-Georg. *Truth and Method*. Translated by Joel Weinsheimer and Donald G. Marshall. Continuum, 1994.

Garnham, Allan. *Mental Models as Representations of Discourse and Text*. Ellis Horwood, 1987.

Gee, James P. *An Introduction to Discourse Analysis: Theory and Method*. Routledge, 1999.

Geeraerts, Dirk, editor. *Cognitive Linguistics: Basic Readings*. Mouton de Gruyter, 2006.

Geeraerts, Dirk, and Hubert Cuyckens, editors. *The Oxford Handbook of Cognitive Linguistics*. Oxford University Press, 2007.

Geuss, Raymond. *The Idea of Critical Theory: Habermas and the Frankfurt School*: Cambridge University Press, 1981.

Giddens, Anthony. *The Nation State and Violence*. Polity Press, 1985.

Goldhammer, Herbert, and Eduard A. Shils. "Types of Power and Status." *American Journal of Sociology*, Vol. 45, no. 2, 1939, pp. 171–182.

Grice, Paul. "Logic and Conversation." *Syntax and Semantics*, Vol. 3. Academic Press, 1975.

Halliday, Michael A.K. "Dimensions of Discourse Analysis: Grammar." *The Handbook of Discourse Analysis,* Vol. 2, Dimensions of Discourse. Academic Press, 1985, pp. 29–56.

Hobbes, Thomas. *Leviathan: Or the Matter, Forme, and Power of a Common-Wealth Ecclesiasticall and Civill,* edited by Ian Shapiro. Yale University Press, 2010.

Hodges, Adam. "The Politics of Recontextualization: Discursive Competition over Claims of Iranian Involvement in Iraq." *Discourse & Society*, Vol. 19, no. 4, July 2008, pp. 483–505, doi:10.1177/0957926508089940.

Hoffman, Stanley. "Discord in Community: The North Atlantic Area as a Partial Integration System." *International Organization,* Vol. 17, Summer 1963, pp. 521–549, doi:10.1017/S0020818300034536.

Holland, Dorothy C., and Naomi Quinn, editors. *Cultural Models in Language and Thought*. Cambridge University Press, 1987.

Johnson-Laird, Philip. N. *Mental Models*. Cambridge University Press, 1983.

Lang, Kurt. "Military Organizations." *Handbook of Organizations,* edited by James G. March, Rand McNally, 1965, pp. 838–878.

Langacker, Ronald W. *Foundations of Cognitive Grammar*. Indiana University Linguistics Club, 1983.

Larrain, Jorge. *The Concept of Ideology*. Hutchinson, 1979.

Lemke, Jay. *Textual Politics. Discourse and Social Dynamics*. Taylor and Francis, 1995.

Marin, Vasile. *Comunicarea în conducerea militară*: Air Forces Academy Publishing House, 2006.

Markman, Arthur B. *Knowledge Representation*. Erlbaum, 1999.

Mills, Wright C. *The Power Elite*. Oxford University Press, 1956.

Moscovici, Serge. *Social Representations: Explorations in Social Psychology*, Vol. 41. Edited by Gerard Duveen, Polity Press, 2000.

Pêcheux, Michel. *Language, Semantics and Ideology*. St Martin's Press, 1982.

Potter, Jonathan. *Representing Reality: Discourse, Rhetoric and Social Construction*. London; Sage, 1996.

Potter, Jonathan, and Margaret Wetherell. *Discourse and Social Psychology: Beyond Attitudes and Behaviour*. Sage, 1987.

Rapoport, Anatol. *Fights, Games and Debates*. University of Michigan Press, 1960.

Reid, Escott. *Time of Fear and Hope: The Making of the North Atlantic Treaty, 1947–1949*. McClelland and Stewart, 1977.

Reisigl, Martin, and Ruth Wodak. *Discourse and Discrimination: Rhetorics of Racism and Antisemitism*. Routledge, 2005.

Rosenberg, Shawn W. *Reason, Ideology and Politics*. Princeton University Press, 1988.

Said, Edward W. *Covering Islam: How the Media and the Experts Determine How We See the Rest of the World*. New York: Pantheon, 1981.

Schank, Roger C., and Robert P. Abelson. *Scripts, Plans, Goals and Understanding: An Inquiry into Human Knowledge Structures (Artificial Intelligence Series)*, 1st ed., Psychology Press, 1977.

Schelling, Thomas C. "The Diplomacy of Violence." *Theories of Peace and Security*, edited by John Garnett, Palgrave Macmillan, 1970, pp. 68–84.

Schiffrin, Deborah. *Approaches to Discourse Analysis*. Blackwell, 1992.

Schmid, Alex P. *Violence as Communication: Insurgent Terrorism and the Western News Media*. Sage, 1982.Shore, Bradd. *Cognition, Culture, and the Problem of Meaning*. Oxford University Press, 1996.

Slater, Phil. *Origin and Significance of the Frankfurt School: A Marxist Perspective*. Routledge & Kegan Paul, 1977.

Snyder, Glenn H. *Deterrence by Denial and Punishment. Research Monograph No. 1*. Center of International Studies, Woodrow Wilson School of Public and International Affairs, Princeton University, 1959.

Stiles, William B. "Qualitative Research: Evaluating the Process and the Product." *Handbook of Clinical Health Psychology,* edited by Susan Llewelyn and Paul Kennedy, John Wiley & Sons, 2003, pp. 477–499.

Thibault, John W., and Harold H. Kelley. *The Social Psychology of Groups.* Wiley, 1959.

Thompson, John B. *Ideology and Modern Culture: Critical Social Theory in the Era of Mass Communication.* Stanford University Press, 1990.

Torfing, Jacob. *New Theories of Discourse: Laclau, Mouffe and Zizek.* Basil Blackwell, 1999.

Van Leeuwen, Theo. "Discourse as the Recontextualization of Social Practice: A Guide." *Methods of Critical Discourse Analysis,* Vol. 2, edited by Ruth Wodak and Michael Meyer, Sage Publications, 2009, pp. 144–161.

Willig, Carla. *Introducing Qualitative Research in Psychology.* McGraw-Hill, 2008.

Wodak, Ruth. "The Discourse-Historical Approach". *Methods of Critical Discourse Analysis* 1, 2001, pp. 63–94.

Wodak, Ruth, editor. *Language, Power and Ideology. Studies in Political Discourse.* John Benjamins Publishing Company, 1989.

Wodak, Ruth et al. *Discourse and Power.* Wien: Deuticke, 1987.

www.ingramcontent.com/pod-product-compliance
Lightning Source LLC
Chambersburg PA
CBHW021149160426
42812CB00078B/343